THE MIND
CONNECTION

THE MIND CONNECTION

How the Thoughts You Choose Affect Your Mood,
Behavior, and Decisions

JOYCE MEYER

NEW YORK · BOSTON · NASHVILLE

Cover design by Jon Richert
Author photograph by David Dobson
Cover copyright © 2015 by Hachette Book Group, Inc.

FaithWords
Hachette Book Group
1290 Avenue of the Americas, New York, NY 10104
faithwords.com
twitter.com/faithwords

Originally published in hardcover and ebook by FaithWords in September 2015.
First Trade Paperback Edition: September 2016

FaithWords is a division of Hachette Book Group, Inc. The FaithWords name and logo are trademarks of Hachette Book Group, Inc.

The publisher is not responsible for websites (or their content) that are not owned by the publisher.

The Hachette Speakers Bureau provides a wide range of authors for speaking events. To find out more, go to www.hachettespeakersbureau.com or call (866) 376-6591.

Library of Congress Cataloging-in-Publication Data has been applied for.

ISBNs: 978-1-4555-1728-2 (trade pbk.), 978-1-4555-1729-9 (ebook)

Printed in the United States of America

LSC-C

10 9 8

CONTENTS

Are your thoughts random and meaningless, or do they affect your life in ways that perhaps you have not yet understood? Do they merely come into your mind from the circumstances and events around you, passing through without meaning and effect, going nowhere and doing nothing, or is it possible that what you think affects how you talk, your attitudes, your decisions, and your emotions? Can your thoughts affect your behavior and even your relationships? I believe they affect how you relate to yourself, to other people, to God, and to all of your circumstances.

Perhaps these are things you have never given any thought to. I know that for most of my life, I certainly didn't. I paid no attention to what I was thinking, and I didn't make the connection between my thoughts and the rest of my life. But the Lord has taught me many things from His Word about the mind connection since those early days, and I'm excited to share those truths with you in the pages of this book.

In the chapters ahead, I want to address three major issues. First, we should understand the power of our thoughts and how they are connected to the way we respond to everything else in life. Second, I strongly desire to show you how to think on purpose instead of having a passive mind. And third, I hope to give you insight on what to do when you feel you have lost control of your thoughts, and how you can regain and maintain the right mental position.

On days when people cannot seem to gain control of their thoughts, they may say something like "I feel like I am losing my mind!" In a way they are, because they seem to be unable to control the thoughts running through it. But when you feel as if you are losing your mind, there are ways to get it back, which I will share with you throughout this book.

Our first impulse is to assume that we are not responsible for what goes through our minds and that there is simply nothing we can do about it, but that is not true. God's Word gives us clear instructions concerning what to think about and what not to think about. It also teaches us that we have the ability to pick and choose, and to keep the good thoughts and cast out the thoughts that poison our lives. We are instructed to cast down wrong imaginations, theories, and reasoning, and lead them away captive to the obedience of Jesus Christ (see 2 Corinthians 10:4–5).

Through studying God's Word, I learned that my thoughts were ruining my life, and if I wanted to enjoy a different quality of life, I had to start controlling them. I began seriously studying God's Word in 1976, and I quickly learned God had a great plan for my life, but I needed to learn how to agree with Him in my thinking in order to have it (see Romans 12:2). I came up with the phrase, "Where the mind goes, the man follows," and I can safely say that if you need a change in any area of your life, it will start with a change in your mind. We have the opportunity to think like God thinks in order to have what God wants us to have, to do what He wants us to do, and to be who He wants us to be.

My first book on the power of thoughts is titled *Battlefield of the Mind*, and the second one is called *Power Thoughts*. Now, in this third one, I hope more than ever before to show the connection between our mind, mouth, moods, and attitudes, among other things. I've written extensively on this topic because I believe with my whole heart that the subject is of vital importance and that our thoughts are, in fact, one of the most difficult areas of life to gain mastery over. We can never learn too much about this all-important subject. You don't have to allow outside forces to control you any longer. With God's help, you can begin doing your own thinking today, remembering that each of your thoughts has some kind of effect on you, your life, and often the people around you.

It is exciting to realize that we can have some measure of control over our words, moods, and attitudes by learning how to think better. We can make ourselves sad, mad, or glad by what we think and how we talk. We can increase or decrease our joy and peace. Think of the mind like the gas tank in your automobile. Your automobile will run well, or perhaps not even run at all, depending on what kind of fuel you put into it. In the same way, when you choose your thoughts carefully, your quality of life will improve in amazing ways. I pray that this will be a life-changing book for you and one that you will read again and again, as well as recommend to your friends.

THE MIND
CONNECTION

SECTION 1

How Your Thoughts Affect Your Outlook on Life

CHAPTER 1

The Life You've Always Wanted to Live

*The thief comes only in order to steal and kill and destroy.
I came that they may have and enjoy life, and have it in
abundance (to the full, till it overflows).*

John 10:10

It was springtime and everything was beginning to blossom. Spring is usually a time of year that people really enjoy. The deadness and cold of winter is over, and spring reminds us of hope and new growth. Julie was doing spring cleaning, changing her closet from winter to spring clothes, and thinking about planting some colorful flowers in the yard. Everything felt bright and filled with hope, but then her husband, Charlie, came home from work with some bad news. He had been fired from his job! Julie found it difficult to have any empathy for him, because this was the fourth job Charlie had been fired from in a seven-year period.

Although Julie was normally very positive and peaceful, the news Charlie brought home was upsetting to her. He told her not to get upset, because he would get another job, but Julie knew there was a deeper problem that Charlie wasn't willing to face and deal with. If he had been fired from one or perhaps even two jobs, she might have agreed that it was simply an irritable boss, or other employee problems—but after four jobs, she knew that somehow Charlie was to blame. Not only had he been fired from four jobs, he was also unable to keep friends. You see, Charlie was very difficult to get along with. He was negative, complained frequently, and had an ability to darken any atmosphere within a few minutes.

Charlie had been angry with his boss, who he said didn't recognize his talents, and Charlie felt certain that he was being treated unfairly. He was angry with his coworkers, because, he said, they didn't like him and had complained to the boss about him. Anger wasn't new to Charlie; in fact, he had been angry about one thing or another for most of his life. He felt that he was not as naturally talented, nor as privileged as most of the people he knew, and he resented it. He often complained that life had dealt him a bad hand. "Life threw me under the bus" was a favorite self-pitying statement of his. He blamed his parents, teachers, and peers for his lot in life. He believed everyone was at fault but him.

Although it was true that Charlie had some disadvantages growing up, he also had the same opportunity that we all do to have and enjoy a good life. I like to say that how we get started in life is not nearly as important as how we finish. Our beginning may not be in our control, but the finish is!

The truth was that Charlie had been fired from his job because he was a very negative-thinking person. He had an entitlement attitude that made him feel he deserved better treatment without doing his part to deserve it. As he stood in the kitchen, telling Julie all about his perceived unfair treatment, he didn't realize he was repeating the same pattern he had followed throughout his life—and he would repeat it again and again unless he was willing to stop blaming everyone else for his problems and take responsibility for the changes that he needed to make.

Enjoying Your Life Begins with a Choice

Although we do not always have the power to change every unpleasant circumstance in our lives, we do have the power to change our outlook. We can look out at life from our inmost being with our hearts filled with positive thoughts and attitudes, or we can respond as Charlie did—allowing the events of life to shape our thoughts and attitudes. This is a decision that only we can make—no one can make it for us!

I firmly believe that the bottom line of what we want from life is to be happy! We want to enjoy it! Sadly, we can waste most of life with the misconception that joy and enjoyment come from our circumstances, but the truth is that they come from our attitude toward each circumstance rather than from the circumstance itself. Obviously, nobody enjoys a troubling or painful circumstance, but if we look at it in a hopeful, faith-filled way, we can watch God work all things out for our good (see Romans 8:28).

Enjoying life begins with the thoughts you choose to think. Yes, it is that simple! No matter what is going on in your life today, if you will choose happy, hope-filled thoughts, you will *feel* happier. Our thoughts are intricately connected to our feelings, so if we want to feel better, we need to think better. Be honest with yourself. Think about what you have been mentally focusing on and how you have been feeling emotionally and even physically. I feel certain you will see a definite connection. Nothing good comes from thinking sour, critical, and negative thoughts, but something good always comes when we think according to God's plan for our life. Of course, you cannot do that if you don't

> Enjoying life begins with the thoughts you choose to think.

know God's plan, so let me take just a few paragraphs to share some of what God's Word teaches.

In the early pages of the Bible, we find this statement:

> *I call heaven and earth to witness this day against you that I have set before you life and death, the blessings and the curses; therefore choose life, that you and your descendants may live.*
>
> Deuteronomy 30:19

It is wise to quickly learn that life offers us blessings and curses, good and evil, and it is our responsibility to choose the good if that is what we want to have. This is what it means to be free! We have free choice, but we should also realize that each choice brings a consequence, and we cannot have one without the other. No matter what happened in your life prior to you being able to make your own choices, the fact is that if you make good choices, the results of those choices will ultimately overturn anything bad that has taken place before. We can overcome evil with good (see Romans 12:21). There are countless testimonies from people who endured horrendous circumstances early in life, but through a strong faith in God, good choices, and hard work have now turned their lives around for the greater good.

God offers each of us an opportunity to have a good life. His promises are for all who will believe! We all believe something, so why not make it something good?

We all believe something, so why not make it something good?

God has promised us salvation, redemption, restoration, joy, peace, His constant presence in our lives, and His power to assist us in all we do. He desires that we enjoy an intimate relationship with Him through Jesus Christ and good relationships with other people. He wants to prosper us, to make us strong in Him, and to see us enjoy our position of right standing with Him through our faith in Jesus. He sets before us life and death, blessing and cursing, and tells us to choose life! We don't even have to figure out what to do—we just need to do what He suggests. Choose life! Choose blessing! Choose good!

Choosing good does not mean that it merely falls on us with no effort on our part, but the effort we make is one that is divinely directed and energized by God Himself. He never asks us to do anything without empowering us to do it.

My father sexually abused me for the better part of about fifteen years. Although my mother was aware of what he was doing, she did nothing to stop it, and that, of course, left me abandoned, abused, lonely, and fearful. Like we all do, I finally grew up and was able to leave home, thinking I had left the problem behind me. However, after suffering mentally, emotionally, and relationally for about twenty-five more years, I learned through God's Word that although I left the problem, the results of it were etched in my soul. The despicable way I had been raised had affected my thinking and, through that, all the other areas of my life. My attitude was much like Charlie's. I was filled with self-pity and anger about my past, totally unaware that it daily affected everything I thought, said, felt, and did. How tragic it is when the answer to our problems is right in front of us, but we either lack knowledge or we are too deceived to see it.

One does not have to endure tragedy in order to develop bad habits in their thought life. I think it is safe to say that most people tend to let outside forces control their thinking instead of generating their own thoughts from within. It is quite possible that most people don't realize that they can choose their own thoughts and make the effort to do exactly that.

I like to say, "Nothing good happens accidently." You can catch disease, but you cannot catch health. In the same way, we cannot catch good thinking, but we can choose it. We will need to choose good, positive, and godly thoughts on purpose every day that we live. I don't think they will ever come so automatically that we never have to put forth an effort. But I do know, from God's Word and experience, that if we leave our minds empty and fruitless, our enemy, the devil, will be more than happy to fill them with every kind of life-stealing thought that exists.

In an effort to show how the enemy attacks our minds, let me share how I just realized that the devil was attacking my mind with negative thoughts while I was trying to write this book instructing others not to do so. The Holy Spirit caused me to recognize that I have been having vague, negative whisperings in my ear all morning that have gone like this: "You don't have the creativity you need today. Just put off writing until tomorrow." The devil is covert and sneaky, so I stopped for a moment and prayed over my mind, asking God to protect it from negative, energy-draining thoughts. The Bible teaches us to cover everything with prayer (see Ephesians 6:18), so that's exactly what I did! You and I can interrupt the devil's plans through prayer. God helped me refocus my mind and convey His message accurately.

We are not beyond the devil's ability to tempt us, but we can always resist him in Jesus' name. There are days when the battle of the mind seems relentless, but victory always comes to those who refuse to give up. Thomas Edison said, "Our greatest weakness lies in giving up. The most certain way to succeed is always to try just one more time."[1] Thankfully, I am pretty familiar with the devil's tactics and have had many years to practice resisting them, but I do realize that for many of you the journey to right thinking is just beginning. I urge you not to be discouraged on the difficult days, because your diligence will pay off with huge benefits in due time. Thomas Fuller said, "All things are difficult before they are easy."[2] Don't be defeated by the difficulty of any task. Any day that we don't give up puts us one day closer to success. Good thinking begins with a choice, so I urge you to make yours today and every day of your life.

> Any day that we don't give up puts us one day closer to success.

Life-Energizing Thoughts

The way to put off your old life and put on the new, enjoyable life that God offers us is by renewing your mind and attitude daily (see Ephesians 4:22–24). "Daily" sounds daunting, doesn't it? Don't you wish Scripture said, "Do this once and you will enjoy victory the rest of your life"? However, it doesn't say that, and if we truly want to live life to the fullest and enjoy each moment of it, we will need to form a habit of thinking life-energizing thoughts instead of life-draining ones. One of the simple ways to practice this is by thinking about what you do have instead of what you don't have, and being grateful for every blessing, no matter how tiny or insignificant it may seem.

Here are some quotes to consider on gratitude:

> If a fellow isn't thankful for what he's got, he isn't likely to be thankful for what he's going to get.
>
> Frank A. Clark[3]

> If you want to turn your life around, try thankfulness. It will change your life mightily.
>
> Gerald Good[4]

The hardest arithmetic to master is that which enables us to count our blessings.

Eric Hoffer[5]

God gave you a gift of 86,400 seconds today. Have you used one to say "thank you"?

William Arthur Ward[6]

An unwillingness to count his blessings was one of Charlie's biggest problems. I think we would all agree that he probably wasn't thankful for much, if anything at all. All of his blessings were clouded by his negative attitude. Instead of thanking God that he had a job, he resented not having a better job. Instead of realizing his parents did their best for him, he believed they didn't love him enough to provide better opportunities. He compared everything about his life to those who had more than he did, but he never realized how much more he had than a majority of people worldwide.

What happened to Charlie in the long run? He did lose one more job and was on the verge of losing another when a Christian man he worked with invited him to go to church with him and his family. Julie already attended church regularly, but Charlie had always refused to go. This time he said yes, and it turned out to be just the right thing at just the right time. He had been miserable long enough; he was finally ready for a change. When the opportunity came at the close of the service to receive Jesus Christ as His Savior, Charlie took a bold step and joined with many others in saying yes to Jesus. Gradually, over the years, as Charlie learned about the new way of thinking and the new life that Jesus offers us, he did change. He and Julie went on to have two amazing children, and Charlie held on to his job and was even promoted several times. I love stories with good endings, don't you? I wish everyone's story ended in victory, but sadly many don't. The opportunity for a great life is available to everyone, but not everyone is willing to do what it takes to have it.

Good things are available to each of us, because God does not play favorites by doing good things for one person and not for another. No matter how bad life has been until now, it can change. Always remember that you can overcome evil with good. The darkness cannot overtake the light as long as we keep the light on. Turn the light on in your mind and fill it with positive, hope-filled, thankful, grateful thoughts. As you do this, you will experience godly energy filling your soul. It will be in your words, your attitudes, and your actions. Everything in life is connected to the mind, and it is there that you win or lose the battle for having the life you have always wanted.

Think About It!

- No matter what you're going through, you have the opportunity to enjoy your life.
- Enjoying your life begins with the thoughts you choose to think.
- Renewing your mind isn't a one-time decision—it is a daily decision to think positive, hope-filled, godly thoughts.
- If you're willing to do what it takes, you can really have a great life, because every part of your life is connected to your mind.

CHAPTER 2

Mind, Mouth, Moods, and Attitudes

You are never too old to set another goal or to dream a new dream.

C. S. Lewis

Would you like to be in a good mood every day? You are probably thinking, *Yes, of course I would. Who wouldn't?* I spent a lot of years being controlled by a variety of moods and believing I had no choice in how I felt. I envied all the "happy people." You know the ones I am referring to; they wake up singing and skip through each day. They are *ALWAYS* happy and don't even have to make an effort to be this way. What is their secret? *Why them and not me?* I used to wonder. Some people are born with a temperament that makes it easy for them to look on the bright side, but even they have to make choices about their thoughts and attitudes toward life. Any person, no matter how naturally inclined they are toward good moods, can have sour, negative thoughts if they don't choose differently.

Your mind, mouth, moods, and attitudes are all intricately connected. First you think, and then your thoughts turn into words that you speak, and the two of them together affect you emotionally and turn into moods and attitudes. If you truly want to be in a good mood on a regular basis, you can start by choosing to think about things that will generate good emotions instead of bad ones.

If you desire greater emotional stability and the ability to maintain a consistent good attitude no matter what your circumstances are, then make it a goal and don't give up until you have reached it. As C. S. Lewis said, "You are never too old to set another goal or to dream a new dream."[1] As you walk with God, you can always begin again. It is never too late for a fresh start. Your history does not have to be your destiny!

Believe

Consistently thinking good and godly thoughts, speaking beneficial words, and enjoying stability in mood and attitude are not necessarily easy things to do, but it is possible. I have personally been working toward this goal for almost forty years, and although I have not arrived at perfection, I have made amazing progress.

For example, Dave no longer has to wonder what kind of mood I will be in when he gets up in the morning. I have successful days, and I also have days when I feel that I failed miserably, but I *believe* that with God's help I can keep growing. I am a goal-oriented person, and accomplishment, even in small doses, motivates me to keep moving forward. I always encourage people to look at how far they have come instead of how far they have to go. The devil wants us to focus on our failures, but God wants us to focus on our successes.

> The devil wants us to focus on our failures, but God wants us to focus on our successes.

A walk begins with one step and then another and another. No matter how long your journey seems, if you take enough steps in the right direction, you will eventually arrive at your desired destination. Don't hesitate to begin because it seems to you that you have a long way to go. It is better to spend your life moving in the right direction one step at a time than to have no direction at all. No matter what your problems may be, things can get better with God's help.

You never have to be afraid to ask God for anything. He is delighted when we ask!

The Word of God tells us:

You do not have, because you do not ask.

James 4:2

Keep on asking and it will be given you; keep on seeking and you will find; keep on knocking [reverently] and [the door] will be opened to you. For everyone who keeps on asking receives; and he who keeps on seeking finds; and to him who keeps on knocking, [the door] will be opened.

Matthew 7:7–8

For this reason I am telling you, whatever you ask for in prayer, **believe** *(trust and be confident) that it is granted to you, and you will [get it].*

Mark 11:24 (emphasis mine)

These Scriptures are an open invitation to experience miracles in your life if you will simply believe. It is important to notice that believing comes before receiving. These verses gives us three steps to answered prayer: ask, believe, and receive. We are not told that we will get what we want or need immediately. The Scripture simply says we will get it. The beginning of prayer is asking, the middle is the waiting and continuing to believe, and the end is the manifestation of the desired result. Those who cannot make it through the middle will never see the miracle! The one thing we need to do in the middle is keep believing that God is working and that our breakthrough may come at any moment.

Believing is a great benefit when it comes to maintaining a good mood and attitude. When you believe, hope comes alive. And one of the great things about hope is that hope brings joy. The apostle Paul said it this way in Romans 5:2:

> *Through Him also we have [our] access (entrance, introduction) by faith into this grace (state of God's favor) in which we [firmly and safely] stand. And let us rejoice and exult in our hope of experiencing and enjoying the glory of God.*

Is there any area of your life in which you have given up hope of seeing change? If so, then may this be a point of resurrection! With God's help, you can resurrect your faith and hope—you can *believe* once again that nothing is beyond God's ability. All things are possible with God!

Take Responsibility

While we are believing and waiting for God to do what only He can do, it is important that we are led by the Holy Spirit in doing whatever God may ask us to do.

We are called to be responsible people who delight in obedience to God. I believe that one of the biggest problems we face in our world today is that many people don't want to take responsibility for their lives. It is easy to think that our problems are someone else's fault, but that mind-set never fixes our problems.

I have watched people with this passive mentality, including my own mother and brother, ruin their lives many times.

Because my mother was passive in dealing with my abusive father, all of our lives were affected in a negative and devastating way. My brother ended up with severe emotional issues that haunted him until he tragically committed suicide. Things could have been different for my brother, but sadly he refused to take responsibility for himself. He always wanted someone else to do for him what he should have been doing himself. He had drug and alcohol abuse problems, and although we tried to help him, there were some choices that only he could make, and he would not make them.

My mother was guilt ridden and lived with so many regrets that she eventually had a nervous breakdown followed by a life-long anxiety disorder. These problems resulted from her unwillingness to confront my dad and stand up for herself and her children. To put it simply, she did not do what she was responsible for doing, and the outcome was that she forfeited the good life that God desired her to have.

When I asked my mother why she stayed with my father, knowing what he was doing to me, she said, "I *thought* I could not financially take care of us, and I didn't *think* that I could face the scandal and what people would *think* if they knew the truth." Her unwillingness to take action ultimately destroyed her life, and it was directly connected to her thoughts.

I know the dangers of passivity because I have watched what it does to people. My mother's passivity and disobedience to God not only did tremendous damage to my brother's life and mine, but it also ruined her life. Jesus teaches us to be responsible, active, alert, energetic, and filled with zeal. Lazy and apathetic people don't win the race or end up with the prize in life.

We may or may not be responsible for the current condition of our lives. Lots of things happen that are out of our control and may not be our fault, but one thing is for sure: We don't have to take it lying down. In other words, we can come against things that are not proper by refusing to let them overwhelm us, and by having an attitude that we will overcome all obstacles with God's help. In order for that to happen, we cannot look at our problems and think, *This will never change,* or *Poor me. Why did this have to happen to me? Now my life is ruined.* We can feel sorry for ourselves and make excuses, but as long as we do, we will not make any progress.

I want to assure you that you do have a choice in what you think. It will take some retraining of the mind and forming new habits, but you can do it with God's help. Please don't wait any longer for someone else to make your life better. Take the responsibility for improving it yourself. Ask God to help you, and then begin following His guidance. I am not suggesting that everything that is wrong will be fixed overnight. As a matter of fact, looking for quick fixes is a deception in itself. Most things take longer than you think they will, and if you're not in it for the long haul, you won't reach your destination.

Stability

One of the things that I appreciate about my husband, Dave, is that he is extremely stable. I never have to wonder what kind of a mood he will be in when he wakes up. This has been important to me, because I grew up in a home that was exactly the opposite. Bad moods were ever present. I'm sorry to say that I learned and then continued the same behavior that I despised. Dave has shared that he remembers driving home from work at night and thinking, *I wonder what kind of mood Joyce will be in tonight?* That is sad, but it was even sadder that I never knew myself. I just went with my feelings, whatever they happened to be. If my circumstances were pleasant and going my way, my mood was good, but Lord help us all if that wasn't the case. Women often control the emotional atmosphere of the home, and I was good at making ours unpleasant. In my defense, let me say that I was deceived through lack of knowledge and that I am extremely and eternally grateful to God for teaching me truth that has set me free.

Like most people, I wasn't fully aware of how bad my attitude was, because I justified it in my own mind by making excuses. I didn't realize how negatively my bad moods were affecting the people around me who loved me. I did know that I was unhappy, and that reality finally opened my eyes to realize that something was wrong. Once I got that far and asked God to show me what was wrong, He answered my prayer. When God began opening my eyes to the truth, I cried for days as I realized how difficult it was for people to be in a relationship with me, and how much of my life I had wasted being in bad moods. At this point, I still wasn't aware that all my moods were connected to my thoughts, but at least I was open to facing truth, and that is the starting point for all personal breakthroughs. If you are not happy and you ask God why, I can promise you that He won't tell you that it is your circumstances. He will tell you that it is your mental and emotional posture toward your circumstances, and you have the opportunity to take responsibility for changing them. He always helps us, but He doesn't do everything for us without any participation on our part.

Be Transformed

Transformation means a thorough change, and that is exactly what Jesus offers us through His death and resurrection. He offers us a new way of living, one filled with good things in which we are not conformed to the world and its superficial, external customs. A new way of thinking and a new attitude will always precede this new way of living. Right thinking and right attitudes are road maps that allow us to reach our destination. Romans 12:2 says:

> Right thinking and right attitudes are road maps that allow us to reach our destination.

> Do not be conformed to this world (this age), [fashioned after and adapted to its external, superficial customs], but be transformed (changed) by the [entire] renewal of your mind [by its new ideals and its new attitude], so that you may prove [for yourselves] what is the good and acceptable and perfect will of God, even the thing which is good and acceptable and perfect [in His sight for you].

In this one Scripture we find the answer to how we can have an enjoyable life that is filled with good things. A good life is not one that is entirely trouble free, but it is one that can always be enjoyed because we trust God and have thoughts filled with hope and a good attitude. Romans 12:2 is a very important verse of Scripture for us to understand. The simplicity of its message is that God has a good, acceptable, and perfect plan for you and me, and the way we can experience that is not to think like the world thinks, but to be changed entirely by learning to renew our mind and think the way God thinks. If you want to have what God wants you to have, learn to think like God thinks.

Mind, mouth, moods, attitudes, and behavior are definitely all connected. Pay particular attention to the thoughts going through your mind, because they will energize the rest of what you do. You can jump-start your day by thinking good things on purpose as one of your first acts of the day. Thinking them and speaking them is the combination I recommend. This exercise only takes a few minutes, but it will be valuable to you all day. You may meditate on and confess things like this:

This is the day God has made, and I am going to enjoy it.
I can handle whatever comes my way today through Christ Who is my strength.
Today, I am energetic and creative.
I have favor with God and man everywhere I go.
Everything I lay my hand to prospers and succeeds.
I enjoy being a blessing to others.
I am thankful for all that God has done for me.
God is working on my problems, and I can wait patiently because His timing is perfect.

A negative mind and mouth will produce negative moods, attitudes, and, in all probability, a miserable day. But the positive approach of setting your mind in an uplifting direction cannot have anything other than a good effect on you and your entire day.

This doesn't mean that you won't have to deal with any unpleasantness throughout the day—and when you do, you may need to make even more choices about how you will think in those situations—but the good news is that you can choose how you will think, the words you want to speak, and the attitude you will have toward life. Your attitude belongs to you, and nobody can force you to have a bad one if you don't want to. Anyone who does have a bad attitude hurts themselves more

Your attitude belongs to you, and nobody can force you to have a bad one if you don't want to.

than anyone, and they hinder any positive progress in their life. A bad attitude and a good life simply don't mix!

Think About It!

- Your mind, mouth, moods, and attitudes are all intricately connected.
- No matter what you experience, you are responsible for your own life.
- A transformed mind leads to transformed moods, attitudes, and behaviors.
- Thinking godly thoughts and speaking them each morning is an exercise that can change your entire day.

CHAPTER 3

How to Think When Life Gets Difficult

Resolve to keep happy, and your joy and you shall form an invincible host against difficulties.

Helen Keller

There is no doubt that thinking positively is much easier when life is not difficult, but it is self-defeating to think that it is impossible. Joy in adversity is a powerful principle that helps us live above the clouds. The sun is always shining somewhere above the storm clouds of life, and if we can see it by faith, we won't cave in to discouraged and depressed thinking.

In Robert Schuller's book *Tough Times Never Last, But Tough People Do*, he tells the following story:

> I remember one winter my dad needed firewood, and he found a dead tree and sawed it down. In the spring, to his dismay, new shoots sprouted around the trunk. He said, "I thought sure it was dead. The leaves had all dropped in the wintertime. It was so cold that twigs snapped as surely as if there were no life left in the old tree. But now I see that there was still life at the taproot." He looked at me

and said, "Bob, don't forget this important lesson. Never cut a tree down in the wintertime." Never make a negative decision in the low time. Never make your most important decisions when you are in your worst mood.

Wait. Be patient. The storm will pass. The Spring will come.

It is more difficult to think and speak positively during the "winters" of our life, but it is helpful to remember that spring always follows winter. A favorite saying in our family is "This too shall pass." Song of Solomon 2:11–12 encourages us to look for springtime during winter when it says: "For, behold, the winter is past; the rain is over and gone. The flowers appear on the earth; the time of the singing [of birds] has come, and the voice of the turtledove is heard in our land."

Winter is merely a time when things are not going well. Perhaps you are having a financial difficulty, relationship problems, or illness. It is not possible to live life and not have winter come around on a regular basis, but it is possible to look for spring in the middle of it. It is very helpful during difficult times to remember that they won't last forever.

Weeping may endure for a night, but joy comes in the morning.
Psalm 30:5b

Have you ever noticed that being upset or downtrodden about problems never changes them? Sometimes we don't take time to look at the fruit of our actions, but if we did, surely we would see that worry is useless. We can learn to enjoy the journey of life, even when it takes us in a different direction than we had planned.

A bad attitude is like a flat tire. If you don't change it, you won't go anywhere. Being worried and upset is like sitting in a rocking chair all day and rocking back and forth. It keeps you busy and eventually wears you out, but it gets you nowhere. Mary Engelbreit said, "If you don't like something, change it; if you can't change it, change the way you think about it."[1] I suggest that if your circumstances don't make you happy, at least let your thoughts do it for you.

> *A bad attitude is like a flat tire. If you don't change it, you won't go anywhere.*

It is very important for each of us to learn how to have the victory in the midst of our problems. God's Word teaches us that we are more than conquerors in the midst of our trials and tribulations (Romans 8:37). When I am in the midst of difficulty, I often turn to Romans 8:35–39, and I remind myself that no matter how difficult life is, God loves me. I try to remember that at times, I may appear as a sheep being led to slaughter, but in the midst of these things, I am more than a conqueror. To me, this simply means that we can always be assured of victory eventually. We may go through very difficult things, but following the principles God has set out for us in His Word will bring us through safely every time.

My Mind Was Kidnapped

During the writing of the first few chapters of this book, I have been experiencing a physical ailment that is making me very uncomfortable. It is one of those "mystery illnesses." You know, the ones the doctor can't explain and no medicine seems to alleviate. I hate those the worst of all, don't you? I can begin to wonder if I am just imagining the symptoms, but the discomfort tells me that I am not. While trying to encourage you about staying positive during difficulty, I went through two days in which I felt as if my mind had been kidnapped. I couldn't seem to focus on much of anything except how I felt, and an inability to focus is not helpful when writing a book.

What did I do? I had to do what I am recommending to you. I kept pressing in and making an effort in God to bring my mind back to what I know to be true in my heart. The Bible teaches us to cast down wrong thoughts (see 2 Corinthians 10:5 KJV), but there are days when I *feel* like I spend the entire day casting them down and they keep coming back. You will experience days like this, and I urge you not to give up on those days and believe you will never be able to think right. Trust me, you are not the only one who has those kinds of days. Just keep saying, "This is an attack, and it will pass." You see, the mind is the battlefield on which we fight against the lies of Satan. Whatever he says is the opposite of what God's Word says, or he may even use Scripture out of context.

When Jesus was enduring His testing and temptation in the wilderness before His public ministry began, the devil said to Him, "If You are the Son of God, throw Yourself down; for it is written, He will give His angels charge over you, and they will bear you up on their hands, lest you strike your foot against a stone" (Matthew 4:6). Satan quoted a Scripture, but used it in a wrong way. Jesus immediately responded, "On the other hand, it is written also, You shall not tempt, test thoroughly, or try exceedingly the Lord your God" (Matthew 4:7). No one can win the battle in their mind unless they know God's Word. The Word of God is Truth, and we can believe that above all else.

I am certain that if I had listened to and followed my thoughts during my two-day struggle, I would have had no authority to write a book on the mind. However, I know from studying Scripture that Satan attacks anytime we try to go forward or do anything good, and that we must stand our ground. When we do, he will eventually go away and wait until a more favorable and opportune time (see Luke 4:13). The apostle Paul said it well when he said, "A wide door of opportunity for effectual [service] has opened to me [there, a great and promising one], and [there are] many adversaries" (see 1 Corinthians 16:9). Anyone who wishes to go through life without any opposition is in for huge disappointment.

Opposition is actually a benefit to us, because it forces us to choose to either use our faith and stand firm in Christ or give up. Each time we make the right choice, it is a little more difficult for the devil to deceive us the next time. He will never stop trying, but we do get better and better at recognizing his attacks and standing against them.

Built for the Battle

God has equipped and anointed us to do hard things. He allows us to go through difficulty to bring glory to Him. He shows Himself strong through us. He told Paul that His strength is made perfect in our weakness (see 2 Corinthians 12:9). We may think we can't make it through difficulty, but those thoughts are inaccurate, according to God's Word. He has promised to never allow more to come on us than we can bear (1 Corinthians 10:13).

During life's difficulties, one of the thoughts that is usually persistent is, *I can't do this; it is just too much; it is too hard.* Watch out for that type of thinking and when you recognize it, remember that it is a lie and replace it with your own God-inspired thought that goes something like this: *I can do what I need to do because God is with me. This winter season in my life will be over and spring will come.*

Perhaps you need to see yourself in a new way. If you are easily disappointed or discouraged, or if you tend to give up easily, realize that you are not alone in your battles. As a matter of fact, your battles belong to the Lord, and He will fight for you as you continue to trust Him. See yourself in Christ, walking with Him in your life instead of being weak and alone.

In the early years of our marriage I was easily discouraged and each time I became that way, the first thing I did was speak negativity out of my mouth. "Nothing ever works right for me," "No matter how hard I try I can't seem to do anything right," or "We will never have any money." My negativity was hard on Dave, but he always remained hopeful and positive. During our difficulties, he remained peaceful and happy, and I, on the other hand, was totally miserable. Life does get difficult at times, but we can learn how to navigate those times successfully without losing our peace and joy. The thoughts we allow into our minds, and the attitudes we choose to have, determine whether we have misery or joy. I am grateful that God has changed me, and if you need a change in this area, He can change you too.

How to Think When a Dream Dies

When one has a dream or goal for their life, and it finally becomes obvious that they need to change directions, it can be depressing or exciting. Many years ago, I tried to be my pastor's secretary. I was told the position just wasn't right for me, and I was let go. I was devastated to say the least, but had I kept the job I thought

I wanted, I wouldn't be doing what I am doing today. When things don't work out the way you planned, you don't have to get discouraged and depressed; instead, you can believe that God has something better for you and get excited to see what it is. Don't be married to your own plan. Man's mind plans his way, but God directs his steps (see Proverbs 16:9).

> *When things don't work out the way you planned… you can believe that God has something better for you and get excited to see what it is.*

Many plans are in a man's mind, but it is the Lord's purpose for him that will stand.

Proverbs 19:21

I used to get very discouraged when my plans didn't work or I didn't reach my goals, but I finally realized that if I truly wanted to serve God with my life, it shouldn't matter what I was doing, as long as it was His plan for me. Perhaps we have too many of our own plans, and it is our own expectations that disappoint us. We can and should still pray, "Your will be done, oh God, and not mine."

One of the ways that we find God's perfect will for us is to step out and find out what works and what does not work. If something doesn't work out, don't give up and waste months in depression; just scratch it off your list of possibilities and go on to the next thing. The choice is yours! I like this quote by Charles Stanley: "Disappointment is inevitable. But to become discouraged, there's a choice I make."[2]

Sometimes I look at finding God's perfect will as trying to find the perfect new outfit. I go shopping and try on different things. I see how they fit and how they look on me. I see if they are comfortable or not. Are they too tight or perhaps too big? I don't get depressed because the first few may not work. I enjoy the shopping trip, and eventually I find the perfect thing that is just right for me. You can look at the dreams you have for your life in a similar way. Keep dreaming and having goals until you find the perfect fit for you!

How to Think in Financial Difficulty

Insufficient funds can pressure the best of us, but we can weather the storm if we think right during the difficulty. Avoid thinking the worst and try thinking the best.

If you have lost your job, then aggressively look for another job, all the time expecting it to be better than the last one.

If you need money, be willing to work at anything until you are able to do what you truly desire to do. When we resist laziness and apathy, God gets on board and makes amazing things happen. My daughter recently told me a story about a man she and her husband met while getting some bids to do some minor home repairs. The man had lost his job seven years ago, but worked at everything from mowing lawns, to cleaning homes, to minor repairs. He has high-level skills in a specific field, but since he was unable to find employment in that field, he determined that he would work at anything and be thankful to get the opportunities he did get. My daughter was amazed at what a good attitude he and his wife had. They ended up feeling led by God to bless the couple financially in a substantial way, but I am sure if he had been bitter and complaining that would not have happened.

I wonder how many blessings and provisions we miss in life because we simply have the wrong attitude. How often is God merely waiting to see how we respond to difficulty before He moves to help us?

I know how frightening it can be when the month is longer than the money, because Dave and I experienced it several times in our lives, but I can truthfully say that God always came through for us. There were times when we had to do without things we wanted. One time we moved to a smaller and more economical apartment. Another time we cut up our credit cards and lived very lean for over a year in order to pay them off. I believe God is always faithful, but He also watches for our faithfulness in being good managers of what we do have.

Think of ways you can save on expenses instead of thinking about all you may have to do without. Think of all the possibilities in front of you instead of what is behind you. Think of ways you can bless someone else, because what we do for others comes back to us multiplied many times over (Luke 6:38). Instead of living in fear due to the economy, live by faith in God and be assured that He is well able to help you.

How to Think When a Relationship Is Difficult

We all run into those times when we are not sure that we can continue in a relationship because of the difficulties we experience getting along together. But I recommend that you avoid thinking, *I am giving up on this person; they are never going to change.* The "never" lie that Satan offers us frequently is just that: *a lie!*

Since all things are possible with God (see Matthew 19:26), there is nobody that is beyond change. Of course, people must be open to changing in order for God to work in their lives, but if they are not, we can even trust God to lead them to be open and willing.

This doesn't mean that we are called upon by God to stay in

abusive or painful relationships, but
since God never gives up on us, we
should not give up on others.

> Since God never gives up
> on us, we should not give
> up on others.

I never gave up the hope that my
father could be saved, and when he
was about eighty years old, he did repent of his sins and receive
Christ as his savior. I saw a genuine change in him. Many of the
years that I was praying for my father, I didn't even see him very
often, but prayer is not hindered by distance.

It is easy to think of all the ways we believe someone else
should change and what they should do to make the relationship
better, but perhaps we should think more about what we might
do to make it better. We always want the other party to change,
but we should also be open to letting God show us ways in which
we might change. Paul wrote to the Romans instructing them to
be adaptable if they wanted to live in unity (see Romans 12:16).
It's good to want peace, but go the extra mile and be the peace-
maker. Don't just think about everything that is wrong with the
person you are struggling with, but also think about their good
points. How we think in relationships is very important, and
right thinking can help make any relationship better.

How to Think About Yourself

God has very good thoughts toward you and it is important that
you learn to think about yourself in the same way that He does.
The Word of God states that two cannot walk together unless
they are agreed (see Amos 3:3), and we cannot walk with God
unless we learn how to agree with Him.

People in general tend to think about all their faults more than they do their strengths, but it is much better to consider both. We don't want to ignore our weaknesses and pretend that they do not exist, but we can become easily discouraged, and perhaps even depressed, if we don't also consider the good things about ourselves.

The apostle Paul warned us not to think more highly of ourselves than we ought to (see Romans 12:3), but he didn't say we are to think "lowly" of ourselves. Think like this: *I have talents, gifts, and abilities that God has given me, and I am thankful for them. I intend to use them for His glory. I also have weaknesses, but I trust God to show His strength through them. Jesus came for weak people, for those who need Him, and I definitely need Him. I am nothing without Christ, and I can do nothing without Him, but I can also do all things through Him.*

Life can get difficult when all we see is everything that is wrong with ourselves and all the things we can't seem to do right. The devil will remind us of them frequently, and for that reason we need to be well educated in God's thoughts toward us and meditate on them often.

Yes, life is often very difficult, but it is not too difficult for the man or woman of God. We are equipped to endure, be steadfast, patient, long-suffering, and joyful in those times. Although life is sometimes difficult, let's not think only of those times. Life is also wonderful, amazing, and an exciting journey, so let's think of the good times more than we think of the bad, because we always overcome evil with good (see Romans 12:21).

Think About It!

- Life does get difficult at times, but we can learn how to navigate those times successfully without losing our peace and joy.

- Opposition is actually a benefit to us, because it forces us to choose to either use our faith and stand firm in Christ or give up.
- When faced with difficulty, choose to think: *I can do what I need to do because God is with me. This winter season in my life will be over and spring will come.*
- If something doesn't work out, don't give up and waste months being discouraged or depressed. Just scratch it off your list of possibilities and go on to the next thing.
- During difficult times, avoid thinking the worst and start thinking the best.

CHAPTER 4

Choose Your Attitude

In every single thing you do, you are choosing a direction.
Your life is a product of choices.

Dr. Kathleen Hall

I came across a story about an incredible choice the community of Newtown, Connecticut, made after the tragic shooting at Sandy Hook Elementary School rocked their community in December 2012. It all started with a family that made an important choice.

When Tim and Julie first heard there was a shooting at a local elementary school, they were naturally concerned. Though their two children were safe in other schools, they had friends with children at Sandy Hook.

As the news broke and the gravity of the situation began to settle in, Tim was reminded of the words of Dr. Martin Luther King Jr.: "Hate cannot drive out hate; only love can do that...I have decided to stick with love. Hate is too great a burden to bear."

With those words fresh in his mind, Tim got on his computer and designed fliers with the words WE ARE SANDY HOOK—WE CHOOSE LOVE.

The message from this simple flier caught on throughout the community. There were even billboards with those words printed on them. The people of Newtown decided to embrace the message. Rather than bitterness or anger, they chose to embrace love and forgiveness in the face of an unspeakable tragedy.[1]

Because of a choice to love, this terrible tragedy at Sandy Hook Elementary was made easier for many of the people. They chose an attitude of love instead of one of hate. I love Dr. King's statement: "Hate is too great a burden to bear." How much better the world would be if more people adopted an attitude of love. We have opportunities on a regular basis to hate, but we may also choose to love. This ability to choose is what makes us free. One right choice can bring multiplied blessings and joy to countless numbers of people, and likewise, one wrong choice can bring pain, tragedy, and untold misery.

The people whose children attended Sandy Hook chose love and restoration, but so many others choose hatred, destruction, and recklessness:

- Hitler chose his destiny, killing millions and finally, himself. Lee Harvey Oswald chose to kill a president and wound a nation. The 9/11 bombers chose a path that changed the world. A bank robber chooses the date, place, and time and robs himself of integrity and his family, and ultimately pays in time behind bars.

But even in the midst of great suffering, good choices can be made. Consider that:

- In World War II, Oskar Schindler saved 1,200 Jews by putting them to work in his factory, spending his entire fortune on bribes and black-market purchases of supplies for his workers to keep them alive until the war's end.[2]

- Abraham Lincoln chose the hard path in freeing a people in bondage.

• Mother Teresa forsook all to help the poor and became a world figure.

The power of choice is quite amazing and has far-reaching effects. We should all give more serious thought to the choices that we make and the impact they have.

Maintaining a Good Attitude

Choosing to live with a good, godly, positive, loving attitude is something that hopefully each of us will do. We should not bounce back and forth between good and bad, godly and ungodly, positive and negative, and love and hate. As God's Word says, "Choose life" (see Deuteronomy 30:19). Choose what will produce life for you and all of those whom you influence throughout your life.

Famed tenor Luciano Pavarotti recalled that his father gave him some very wise advice regarding the power of choice. When Pavarotti was young, he worked diligently under the tutelage of Arrigo Pola to develop his voice. However, he also enrolled in a teachers college, not sure if music would pan out as a career. Upon graduation, Pavarotti was unsure which career to pursue—music or teaching.

He asked his father, "What should I do? Should I sing or teach?" His father replied with these words: "If you try to sit on two chairs, you will fall between them. For life, you must choose one chair."

Even though it took him several more years of continued practice and hard work before he made his first professional appearance, Luciano Pavarotti never regretted his decision to pursue music wholeheartedly. He would say later in life, "Commitment, that's the key. Choose one chair."[3]

Luciano was choosing a career and we are choosing an attitude to live with, but the principle is the same. It is unwise to be content to have a good attitude only when things are to our liking, and then transition to a bad attitude when they aren't. It takes no courage or real strength to have a good attitude when things are good, but to maintain one throughout life no matter what our circumstances are, that takes a strong commitment.

It is exciting to me to know that I can choose my attitude. My gender is chosen for me; I have no choice in my eye color, my height, and many other things, but my attitude is something I can choose. Good thoughts always precede a good attitude, and we cannot have one without the other. A good attitude makes life seem good even if it is difficult. People may wonder how you could possibly be happy with the troubles you have, but your secret is simply maintaining a good attitude. An attitude that says things will be made right in the end. An attitude that is hopeful when others are giving up.

You may be thinking, *Well, that sounds nice, but it is very hard to do.* Actually, it is harder on us to have a bad attitude than a good one. I watched my father have a bad attitude all of his life, and he was one of the most unhappy and miserable human beings I ever knew. His inner thought life and the resulting attitude left him with a continual scowl on his face. Even when he answered the phone with "Hello," he sounded as if he was irritated that he had to do so. Not everyone with a sour attitude is as negative as he was, but to have one at all is never productive.

Our attitude actually affects our posture and facial expressions. Let's say that someone we will call Ruth needs to clean her house on Monday, but she doesn't want to do it. It is actually foolish to have a bad attitude about something we have to do anyway. As long as we are going to do it, why not do it with a good attitude so we can find some joy in doing it? But Ruth had not come to that realization yet. She had the habit of letting her thoughts and emotions run rampant and control her attitude.

Ruth cleans, but she does it with a disgusted look on her face and with her shoulders slumped over, clearly expressing her dislike for the task at hand. All day she thinks about how hard she is working and how she wishes she could be out with friends having a good time, or lying on the sofa watching television.

Ruth had a spacious and beautiful home that she should have been expressing gratitude to God for as she cleaned. She could have been enjoying all the nice things God had provided for her, but she was blinded by her bad attitude and self-pity. Her mood got worse as the day went by, because attitudes and moods are connected. By the time her family got home, she was so upset that she began to find some fault with each family member. She told her husband that he didn't help her enough, even though he had a job that required a lot of him physically. She told her son that he was always messy and only made more work for her. Her daughter was chastised for not trying harder in school. Even the dog got into trouble for getting water on the floor while trying to drink!

I well remember days like this when I let a self-centered, self-pitying attitude ruin my day and cause me to be cranky with my family. I can assure you that whatever I have to do to maintain a good attitude now is worth it. It is easier on my health and everyone around me, as well as making life enjoyable.

Attitudes to Avoid

Because I have a lot of experience with self-pity, it is one of the attitudes I definitely avoid, and I encourage others to do the same thing. Self-pity is truly pitiful; it is actually idolatry, because we are turning inward and idolizing ourselves.

Self-pity is truly pitiful.

We think incessantly about ourselves and all the ways in which we are mistreated or disadvantaged. If we truly look at what others have, there are plenty who probably have much less than we do. When we allow our mind to rotate round and round on all the things we don't like about our lives, we have no peace of mind.

I read about a study Duke University did on the subject of peace of mind. There were several factors listed that contributed to mental and emotional stability, but two things really caught my attention: choosing not to waste energy fighting against things you cannot change and refusing to live in self-pity. Both of these decisions helped foster peace of mind and contributed to a happier life.[4]

Your life may not be perfect, and perhaps you're not as appreciated as you should be, but feeling sorry for yourself will never change it. Use your energy for something useful instead of useless. Self-pity is a trap. It is like being in a prison in solitary confinement. All that is in our thinking is how bad off we are. We live in the darkness of selfishness and fail to see how truly blessed we are in many ways.

An impatient attitude is another bad attitude to avoid. It brings a lot of stress into our lives, because the simple truth is that we all have to wait on things we want and desire, so we might as well learn to wait patiently. Here is a short story that gives us a hint about how to do it.

A man observed a woman in the grocery store with a three-year-old girl in her basket.

As they passed the cookie section, the little girl asked for cookies and her mother told her no. The little girl immediately began to whine and fuss. The mother said quietly, "Now, Monica, we just have half of the aisles left to go through; don't be upset. It won't be long."

Soon they came to the candy aisle, and the little girl began to shout for candy. And when told she couldn't have any, she began to cry. The mother said, "There, there, Monica, only two more aisles to go, and then we'll be checking out."

When they got to the checkout stand, the little girl immediately began to clamor for gum and burst into a terrible tantrum upon discovering there would be no gum purchased. The mother patiently said, "Monica, we'll be through this checkout stand in five minutes and then you can go home and have a nice nap."

The man followed them out to the parking lot and stopped the woman to compliment her. "I couldn't help noticing how patient you were with little Monica," he said. Whereupon the mother said,

"I'm Monica...my little girl's name is Tammy." (author unknown)

Sometimes we have to talk to ourselves during difficulty in order to keep convincing ourselves that we can be patient and make it through the difficulty. The fruit of patience is in us as children of God, but we do have to use self-control in order for it to manifest. If we say the first thing that comes to our mind (never a good idea), it's likely we won't be glad to wait. The flesh is just impatient, but thankfully it can be controlled and even retrained.

Some people think one step ahead of where they actually are, which can cause frustration. One of the best ways to be patient is to keep your mind focused on what you are currently doing. Don't be so focused on the destination that you fail to enjoy the journey. We live in a fast-paced society where everything moves quickly, and it is easy to get caught up in the cycle of "hurry."

However, it is not good for us, and it usually ends up causing us to have a short fuse when things don't go our way. It doesn't take much imposition or inconvenience to make us blow up!

They say that practice makes perfect, so let's practice having a patient attitude with situations, people, and ourselves. Most of all, let's be patient with God when we are waiting on Him to do something we have asked Him to do. God has a perfect timing for all things, and He will not be rushed, so settle down and enjoy the wait.

> God has a perfect timing for all things, and He will not be rushed, so settle down and enjoy the wait.

Don't slip into a "This is too hard—I can't do it" attitude. Only a very weak person decides something is too hard before they have even tried to do it. Or perhaps they do try a couple of times and then they give up. Even that is less than God's best because His Word tells us not to get weary in doing what is right, because in due time we will reap if we don't faint and give up (see Galatians 6:9). The fainting actually takes place in our minds, and then our will to succeed goes right down the drain.

No one can succeed if they don't think they can. Maintaining an "I can" attitude is the forerunner to the completion of any project. It would be amazing if we could count up all the missed opportunities some people have in a lifetime simply because they think the work or sacrifice involved in doing a thing would be "too hard."

The list of attitudes we should avoid could go on and on. Others we might consider are a complaining attitude, a selfish attitude, a jealous attitude, a stubborn attitude, or a lazy attitude. In short, we should work with God toward keeping a godly and positive attitude at all times. Positive things add to our lives, and negative ones subtract, so let's be wise enough to make the better choice. Choose your attitude wisely, because, as it has been said, it does determine your altitude. Nobody with a bad attitude is going to go very far in life, nor will they be happy.

I heard a story about a ninety-two-year-old woman who was being moved to a nursing home after her husband of seventy years passed away. She waited many hours in the lobby as the facility staff made all the arrangements and prepared her room.

Because this elderly woman was legally blind, a kind staff member described the room in great detail as final preparations were being made. "I love it already!" the new patient exclaimed.

"How can you love it? You haven't even been in the room yet," the staff member said.

And that's when this woman said something truly extraordinary: "That doesn't have anything to do with it. Happiness is something you decide on ahead of time."[5] I love that attitude, don't you? It didn't matter how the furniture was arranged or where the room was located; she had already made a choice—the same choice you and I can make today. Let's choose to be happy!

Think About It!

- The attitude you choose goes a long way in determining the life you are going to live.
- It's actually harder to have a bad attitude than a good one.
- Don't be so focused on the destination that you fail to enjoy the journey.
- You can practice having a patient attitude and thinking God-honoring thoughts.
- An "I can" attitude is key to the successful completion of a project.

CHAPTER 5

Anyone Can Be Happy

Do not abandon yourself to despair. We are the Easter people and hallelujah is our song.

Pope John Paul II

There is a great deal of sadness in the world that could be avoided if people would learn to think the way God instructs us to think. We can actually make ourselves happy if we know how to do it and are willing. Most of us have thought ourselves out of happiness countless times, so why not start thinking ourselves into it? Henri Nouwen said, "Joy does not simply happen to us. We have to choose joy and keep choosing it every day."[1] If we choose to worry and imagine the worst of what could happen, then we lose the opportunity for happiness. I've heard it said that children are happy because they don't have a file in their minds called "All the things that could go wrong."

I am sure you have heard the statement "Perception is everything," and it really is true to a large degree. How we see things affects our moods and determines whether we will be sad or joyful. If someone doesn't like me, but I believe they do, then I am affected by what I believe, not by their opinion of me.

I am not suggesting that we never face reality. Facts are facts, but the truth, which God reveals to us through studying His

Word, can change facts. We can choose to follow God's advice and believe the best about our current reality, and by doing so we will remain happy while God is working all things out for our good (see Romans 8:28). Dale Carnegie said, "It isn't what you have, or who you are, or where you are, or what you are doing that makes you happy or unhappy. It is what you think about."[2]

> Folks are usually about as happy as they make their minds up to be.
>
> Abraham Lincoln[3]

> It's been my experience that you can nearly always enjoy things if you make up your mind firmly that you will.
>
> L. M. Montgomery, *Anne of Green Gables*[4]

We can see from these quotes and others like them that people throughout history have discovered the impact thoughts have on happiness.

The Value of Joy

Joy is extremely valuable. The Bible states that the joy of the Lord is our strength (see Nehemiah 8:10)! Don't give yours away too easily.

At what price are you willing to sell your joy? In his book *I Once Was Blind But Now I Squint*, Kent Crockett tells the story of his wife accidentally pulling up to the full-service pump rather than the self-service pump at a gas station. She didn't realize that she was now paying an extra fifty cents per gallon for the increased service.

When she got home and told her husband she had paid seven dollars more than she wanted to, he was upset at the increased cost. He did the math in his head and deduced they could have taken their car 128 more miles had they only paid for self-service. He was angry that the gas station had charged so much more for full service.

But then a realization hit him. He said that God showed him that he had sold his joy for seven dollars! Surely his joy was more valuable than that.[5]

This is a very impactful story that leaves me wondering how often I have sold my joy for even less. Jesus said that He left us His joy.

> *And now I am coming to You; I say these things while I am still in the world, so that My joy may be made full and complete and perfect in them [that they may experience My delight fulfilled in them, that My enjoyment may be perfected in their own souls, that they may have My gladness within them, filling their hearts].*
>
> John 17:13

We have joy in us as a gift from Jesus, but we don't always appropriate and use all that we have. Can joy be blocked and hindered by life's difficulties? The answer is yes it can be, but it doesn't have to be. It all depends on what we choose to focus on.

> *I have told you these things, so that in Me you may have [perfect] peace and confidence. In the world you have tribulation and trials and distress and frustration; but be of good cheer [take courage; be confident, certain, undaunted]! For I have overcome the world. [I have deprived it of power to harm you and have conquered it for you.]*
>
> John 16:33

Difficulty is never enjoyable, but right thinking in the midst of it will cheer us up. Even though we have trials, we can face them with courage, being confident of God's love and His promise to help us. It seems to me that joy and happiness (which is a part of joy) comes more from what we believe than from what is happening to us.

Would you be willing to make some changes in your approach to life and even develop some new habits if it would enable you to have more joy and enjoyment?

Perhaps if we studied the habits and attitudes of happy people we could see some of the things we might need to change if we truly want to be happy. If we value joy, then we cannot just passively sit and wish to be happy; we can aggressively pursue it and be willing to make adjustments where they are needed.

One of the things I learned during my pursuit to be happy was that I could not give someone else the responsibility for my joy. First, it is not fair to them and, second, they have no capability to do so all the time. God wants us, first and foremost, to find our joy in Him, and He won't allow us to constantly get it from any other source. If we were able to do that, we would depend on those people in a way that only belongs to God. Certainly, people can do things that make us happy, but our experience proves that they also disappoint us. The next time you find that you are angry with someone because they didn't make you happy, you might want to adjust your attitude and take responsibility for your own joy.

Another thing I learned was that complication and stress were devastating to my joy, and the only way to lessen them was to work at simplifying my life. You may think this is impossible for you to do, but it really isn't. If we do the things God has truly assigned us to do, He always gives us the grace to do them peacefully and joyfully. However, if we complicate life by adding all the things that people expect us to do, the story changes. Our approach to life is very important. Try the simple approach!

1. If someone hurts your feelings or disappoints you, choose to forgive them instead of getting angry.
2. If things don't work out your way, trust that God is in control and that what He does will be better than what you had planned.
3. When a problem arises, believe the best instead of the worst.
4. Don't waste your energy worrying because it doesn't do any good.
5. Don't buy more than you can comfortably pay for.
6. Be your unique self and never compare yourself with anyone else.
7. When you sin against God, repent, receive your forgiveness, and don't waste time feeling guilty.
8. When someone doesn't like you, pray for them. The real problem may be that they don't like themselves.
9. If your schedule is overcrowded, then change it!
10. If you're tired all the time, then get more rest.

The simple approach to pressing problems leaves room for joy in the midst of them, and they get solved much quicker.

Take some time to pray and ask God to begin showing you things you could change that would increase your joy. It has been said that only a fool expects to keep doing the same thing over and over and get a different result.

"If" and "When"

In her blog article "The Psychology of Happiness," Kim Gaines Eckert, a Christian counselor, talks about how people think they will be happy "if":

> *If* I can just find the right person and get married, then I will be happy... *if* I could get that new house or new car or new boat or new job... *if* I could just get pregnant and have a baby... *if* I could have another baby... *if* I could quit my job and stay home with my kids... *if* we could move closer to family and have help... *if* I could lose 15 pounds... *if* I could travel more... *if* we could afford to retire.

I mentioned earlier that Satan offers the "if lies" to our minds, hoping we will always wait to be happy some other time. He knows the value of true joy, and it is dangerous to him.

Eckert also said that when we get those things we thought would make us happy, we are happy, until we're not. I love that statement. She shares that psychologists call this the "hedonic treadmill," in which the efficacy of a new pleasure wears off over time. The more feel-good stuff we do or have, the more we need in order to achieve the same level of happiness.[6] It's like the tolerance that develops over time in addictions, so we need three of something now instead of the two that once satisfied us.

Detox Your Brain

If you have a long-standing habit of thinking thoughts that poison or kill your joy, then you may need a brain detox. Detoxing is fairly popular these days. Doctors and nutritionists have discovered that a lot of illness results from toxins that are lodged in our bodies and need to come out. This is accomplished in various ways, but all in all, the results are amazing for many people. Detoxing the brain by replacing toxic thoughts with healthy ones also has an amazingly good effect in every area of our lives. Dr. Caroline Leaf shares it this way:

> Medical research increasingly points to the fact that thinking and consciously controlling your thought life is one of the best ways, if not the best way, of detoxing your brain. It allows you to get rid of those toxic thoughts and emotions that can consume and control your mind.

I find it interesting that medical and scientific research have taken centuries to discover what God told people from the beginning of time. We have been given the mind of Christ and that means that with His help we can think as He would think (1 Corinthians 2:16). Dr. Leaf goes on to say:

> Change in your thinking is essential to detox the brain. Consciously controlling your thought life means not letting thoughts rampage through your mind. It means learning to engage interactively with every single thought that you have, and to analyze it before you decide either to accept or reject it.
>
> How do you go about doing that? By "looking" at your mental processes. That may sound like a strange if not impossible thing to do. After all, it's not as if you can just crack open your skull like an egg and have a look at what is going on inside your brain.

It is possible, however, to look at your mental processes. In fact, it is not just possible, it is essential.

For example, consider the following:

How many "could-have," "would-have," "should-have" statements have you made today?

How many "if onlys" were part of your inner vocabulary today?

How many times have you replayed in your head a conversation or situation that pained you, or one that hasn't even occurred yet?

How many scenarios have you created of the unpredictable future?

How much is speculation taking out of your day?

How passive is your mind?

How honest are you with yourself?...

How distorted is your thinking? Are you forming a personal identity around for example, a disease? Do you speak about "my arthritis," "my multiple sclerosis," "my heart problem"?

Do you ever make comments like "nothing ever goes right for me"; "everything I touch fails"; "I always mess up"?

If you answered yes even to just one of these, your brain needs detoxing right now.[7]

That means you need to start replacing wrong thoughts with right ones, or another way I like to say it: "Start replacing your old thoughts with God's thoughts found in His Word." This, of course, is a process that in reality goes on throughout our lifetime, but each toxic thought that is replaced with a healthy one releases more joy into our life, as well as health into our body.

In my book *The Secret to True Happiness* I share some key points, and I would like to mention three of them in this book.

Put God First:

I don't know how anyone can be consistently happy if they don't believe in God. Oddly enough, some people who don't believe make it their mission in life to try to diminish the faith of others. They are unhappy and they want to make others unhappy too.

A story is told of a lady who had to travel extensively for her business, and most of her travel involved flying. But flying made her very nervous, so she always took her Bible to read on long flights, because it helped her relax.

On one trip, she was sitting next to a man. When he saw her pull out her Bible, he gave a little chuckle and a smirk, and went back to what he was doing. After a while, he turned to her and asked, "You don't really believe all that stuff in that book, do you?" The lady replied, "Of course I do. It's in the Bible."

He said, "Well, what about that guy who was swallowed by the whale?" She replied, "Oh, Jonah. Yes, I believe that story. It is in the Bible." He asked, "Well, how do you suppose he survived all that time inside a whale?" The lady said, "Well, I don't really know. I guess I will ask him when I get to Heaven."

"What if he isn't in Heaven?" the man asked sarcastically.

"Then *you* can ask him!" replied the lady.

I can safely say that the man in this story was not a happy man. I can sense the bitterness in his comments and questions. It is a terrible tragedy when one finds it difficult to believe.

Believe like a little child and put God first in your life, and happiness will be more easily attained. God is the source of all good things, and that includes joy. Jesus said He came that we might have and enjoy our lives in full measure (John 10:10). I recommend starting each day talking with God about your day and asking for His help in all that you need to do.

It was quite life-changing for me when I realized that God wants each of us to be thoroughly happy and to fully enjoy life. I had grown up without enjoying much of anything, and I never really had the opportunity to be a carefree child. Thankfully, God has given me the opportunity to be one as an adult. Believe that God loves you, He is for you, He is with you, and He delights in helping you. Feel free to talk to Him about anything, because He is interested in everything about you. He wants to hear you laugh and see you enjoying your life.

Know Who You Are:

As a child of God, it is important to understand that you become a new creature in Christ when you receive Him as your Savior and Lord.

> Therefore if any person is [ingrafted] in Christ (the Messiah) he is a new creation (a new creature altogether); the old [previous moral and spiritual condition] has passed away. Behold, the fresh and new has come!
>
> 2 Corinthians 5:17

I love new beginnings, and that is what Jesus offers us. No matter what you may have done wrong in your past, you are now a new creation. Old things have passed away and all things are made new. That truth alone should make us very happy!

Jesus took all of our sin upon Himself and gave us His very own righteousness. Through Him we have right standing with God. God now sees us as being right with Him. We no longer need to feel "wrong" about ourselves.

For our sake He made Christ [virtually] to be sin Who knew no sin, so that in and through Him we might become [endued with, viewed as being in, and examples of] the righteousness of God [what we ought to be, approved and acceptable and in right relationship with Him, by His goodness].

2 Corinthians 5:21

Reading this Scripture should make us laugh out loud. What good news! We are made right with God, approved by and acceptable to Him. Amazing! If you have felt bad about yourself, wished you were someone else more acceptable, or compared yourself with other people, those days are over if you know who you are in Christ. He gives us a new identity, and all we need to do is believe it and receive it by faith!

Know the Power That Is Yours as a Believer:

Feeling incapable, unable, and overwhelmed hinders our happiness, but God has solved that problem for us if we will only believe it. The apostle Paul prayed for the church asking that they might know the power available to them as believers (see Ephesians 1:19). If we think we are incapable, then we will be, and if we think we cannot handle our challenges in life, then we won't. Our thoughts affect us in astounding ways. They are a key in regulating our energy levels. Think weak and be weak…think strong and be strong! We are strong

> *Think weak and be weak… think strong and be strong!*

in Christ, not in ourselves. When you need to do anything, don't look to yourself and ask if you are able—look to Jesus and know that in Him you are able. Here is God's promise to you:

*Behold! I have given you authority and power to trample
upon serpents and scorpions, and [physical and mental
strength and ability] over all the power that the enemy [pos-
sesses]; and nothing shall in any way harm you.*

Luke 10:19

Anyone can be happy if they believe right and think right! Let
us make a commitment to think like God thinks so we can be the
people He wants us to be and live the joy-filled life He purchased
for us with the life of His Son Jesus Christ.

Think About It!

- If we value joy, then we cannot just passively sit and wish to
  be happy; we must aggressively pursue it and be willing to
  make adjustments where they are needed.
- You cannot give someone else the responsibility for your joy.
  It is a choice you have to make.
- Simplifying your life is a great way to increase your joy.
- Believe like a child and put God first in your life, and happi-
  ness will be more easily attained.

CHAPTER 6

The Power of Focus

*Concentrate all your thoughts upon the work at hand. The
sun's rays do not burn until brought to a focus.*

Alexander Graham Bell

If you want to do one thing, but you have your mind on something
else, you limit your power and ability. Learning to focus is
perhaps one of our greatest challenges in the world today.

No horse gets anywhere until he is harnessed.
No steam or gas drives anything until it is confined.
No Niagara is ever turned into light and power until it
is tunneled.
No life ever grows great until it is focused, dedicated,
disciplined.

Henry Emerson Fosdick[1]

In order for me to do a good job writing this book, I have to
shut out everything else and focus. I need to be alone and without
distractions. At times I have to make difficult choices in order
to be able to fulfill the call on my life. I recently got a new puppy,
because my dog I had for twelve years died. Not having had a
puppy for a long time, I had forgotten how much work they are.
Not only that, but the puppy I got was as feisty as she could be.

Actually, she had a mind of her own and wasn't too keen on obedience, even though I had sent her for three rounds of extensive
training. By the time she was eight months old, I finally had to
face facts. She was not the right dog for me because I could not
focus properly on the work God has called me to and still take
care of her. I made the difficult choice not to keep her.

A few months went by and I decided to try another puppy,
and the one I got that time was sweet, cuddly, and obedient; she
learned quickly and was very cute! (Cute is important!) But even
taking care of her was challenging due to my travel and schedule.
However, my daughter offered to share the duties of "dog parent-
ing" with me, and it is now a perfect situation. I have the dog
anytime I want her, and I take her home when I don't. Perhaps
God blessed me with an absolutely perfect situation because I
was willing to sacrifice my desire in order to stay focused on His
will for my life. Always remember that God promises to give us
the desires of our heart if we will delight ourselves in Him (see
Psalm 37:4). Even if you have to let go of something you would
like to have or do, God is able to replace it with something better
than you could imagine.

Focus requires understanding that you can have too many
top priorities, or nothing becomes a top priority. When we do
too many things at once, we end up doing nothing well.

> When we do too many things at once, we end up doing nothing well.

If you have a goal, something you
truly want to accomplish, you will
need to focus your thoughts, ener-
gies, and time toward that thing. It is useless to "wish" you could
do something; if you truly desire to do something, you must focus
and do it! I have written over a hundred books throughout the
past thirty-five years, because I feel that God wants me to leave

a legacy to the body of Christ. Naturally, I have had to sacrifice other things in order to accomplish this, but I don't feel deprived. I actually feel fulfilled, because I believe I have done what I was intended to do.

The world is filled with dissatisfied, unfulfilled people, and I suspect it is due to them not giving themselves to what they were meant to do. God has given each of us gifts and abilities, and we should nourish and develop them. Paul wrote to the Romans telling them to give themselves to whatever their gift was (see Romans 12:6–8). I am gifted as a public speaker, but I am not gifted as a musician. I tried in the earlier years of my life to learn to play guitar, but it was a waste of time. We cannot accomplish a thing merely because we want to do so. God only helps us do what He wants us to do. Find out what that is and give yourself to it.

The writer of Ecclesiastes said we are to give our mind to what we are doing (see Ecclesiastes 5:1). I don't know about you, but I often find that difficult. My mind has a tendency to wander, and I have to keep calling it back to what is at hand. The more we allow our minds to run wild, the wilder they will become, but they can be trained to focus with some diligent effort. You will never control your thoughts if you don't believe that you can. At any moment you can stop thinking about something you don't want to think about and start thinking about something you want to think about. I tell people, "If you don't want to think about something, then think about something else."

It is also possible to keep your mind on one thing at a time, but it does take practice.

Richard Carlson said in *Don't Sweat the Small Stuff...and It's All Small Stuff*, "When you do too many things at once, it's impossible to be present-moment oriented. Thus, you not only lose out on much of the potential enjoyment of what you are doing, but you also become far less focused and effective."

Reprioritize

Keeping our priorities in proper order is very important, and I have found that in order to do so, I have to make changes and adjustments fairly frequently. Life seems to get too full sometimes without me even knowing how it got that way. We say yes to one thing and then another, we do a friend a favor, we feel we should attend an event because we don't want anyone to be offended, and on and on it goes. We don't thoroughly think through what each thing we commit to will require of us, or how much time and energy it will take, and soon we feel pressured. We are frustrated because we are not getting the things done that we know we should be doing, and find ourselves doing many things we don't even really want to do.

When that happens, it is time to reprioritize. We make our schedules, and we are the only ones who can change them.

Are you willing to make a change? I often ask people that question, because some things will never change unless we change them. It is useless to complain about something if you could change it and aren't willing to do so. More important than the many things we try to cram into our day is whether or not we have peace. If we have no peace,

> It is useless to complain about something if you could change it and aren't willing to do so.

then we have no power. All we have is frustration, complication, and a lot of unfinished projects.

If you are looking through a camera lens and what you see is out of focus, you take time to refocus the lens before taking the picture. We should do the same thing with our life if our priorities have gotten out of focus. See your mind as the camera lens, and adjust your thinking so you are putting your energies into what you truly know you want to do.

God's Word speaks about the need to focus frequently, so it must be important. The apostle Paul had a goal, and he knew that he had to keep pressing toward it. I am sure he had many requests made of him and expectations placed on him, but in the midst of it all, he managed to focus on his main goal, which was spiritual maturity (see Philippians 3:10–14). Paul wanted to be what God wanted him to be! The church is filled with people who want to be strong against temptation, and yet they never make studying God's Word a priority, so they fail time and time again.

The author of Hebrews said to look away from all that would distract them unto Jesus, who is the Leader and Source of our faith (see Hebrews 12:2). Always keep Jesus in the center of all that you do, and refuse to let anything distract you from Him.

Paul wrote to the Romans and told them to set their minds on, and seek those things, that gratify the Spirit (see Romans 8:5). We must first set our mind in the right direction before we can go in the right direction. Focus requires that we set our minds and keep them set on what is important to us at any given time. Distractions are abundant. The devil uses them to keep us from bearing good fruit and being fulfilled, but with God's help and some determination, we can focus!

Don't be discouraged if you frequently find that you have allowed your priorities to get out of line—just refocus and get back on track. Be determined to finish the things you start and give yourself to what you truly want to do.

A Disciplined Mind

Scripture tells us that God has given us a sound mind, and that is a mind of discipline and self-control (see 2 Timothy 1:7). I am glad to know that I have one, but like most of us I am still developing it. I have to be honest and say that giving myself to the thing I am currently doing can be very challenging at times, and I pray daily that God will help me focus. My mind tends to be busy and is often a step ahead of where I am. My children tease me because I have been known to start opening the car door to get out of it before the car has come to a full stop. Yesterday I was rinsing my mouth with mouthwash and got distracted and swallowed it! (Not tasty!) Learning to enjoy and be fully present in the moment is a challenge for me, but it is one I am not going to give up on. I have experienced the power of focus, and I also know the misery of being scatterbrained, and I am not going to settle for anything less than focused thinking. The greatest moment in our lives is the present moment! We need to live it fully and enjoy it completely.

> Let your eyes look right on [with fixed purpose], and let your gaze be straight before you.
>
> Proverbs 4:25

The less noise we have around us, the easier it is to focus. I usually try to get by myself for large chunks of time when I write my books, but on this writing trip, several of my family members are with me. I am in a room by myself, but I can hear them in the other part of the house. I hear laughter and wonder what is so funny, and then I am tempted to go out and see what is going on. If I do, then I break my focus and it takes time for me to get refocused again.

We cannot always be hermits, but there is nothing wrong with needing time alone to focus on what is important to you.

What If I Miss Out on Something?

I think we get sidetracked often simply because we want to be involved in everything that is going on. We don't want to miss anything! I hear the laughter and think, *I want to be part of the fun*. But when my book is published, those having fun may wish they had written a book. We simply cannot do everything. We must choose what is most important to us and focus on that.

To be able to focus means that I have to say no to many other things. Some of the things I say no to may be things I would like to say yes to. However, when I compare them to my main goals in life, I find I still need to say no. The simplest form of what I am presenting is that you cannot have everything you want and have anything worth having. Making wise choices is the key to success. Choose to do now what you will be satisfied with later on. If I choose to leave my writing and go see what the laughter is all about, it might be fun right now, but I can assure you that later when I have not reached my goal for the day, I will be sorry I did it. The only way to live without regrets is to do what you know you should do, when you know you should do it.

The Mind-set of a Champion

Often called the former best woman soccer player in the world, Mia Hamm says she's often asked, "Mia, what's the most important thing for soccer players to have?" With no hesitation, she answers, "Mental toughness." And she doesn't mean some innate trait. When eleven players want to knock you down, when you're tired or injured, and the referees are against you, you can't let any of it affect your focus. How do you do that? You have to learn how. "It is," says Hamm, "one of the most difficult aspects of soccer and the one I struggle with every game and every practice."[2]

It is impossible to be a champion at anything without the power of focus, and it is never something that comes without oppo-

> It is impossible to be a champion at anything without the power of focus.

sition. I have watched golf matches and noticed that the champions are the ones who don't let a bad shot make them angry. They know they must stay focused if they are to have any hope of winning. I have watched football players get knocked down, and baseball players fall down, but the great ones don't focus on the fall; they focus on winning the game. Focus requires getting right up after a fall and going on as if nothing had happened. Champions have no time to wallow in their mistakes.

Whether it is a champion golfer, a champion mom, or a champion teacher, it is imperative that we learn to focus on what is at hand, and that means letting go of past (no matter how recent) mistakes.

I have also learned that successful sports stars always play the game in their mind before they play it in reality. I know a former quarterback who spent entire days laying out plays and going over and over them in his mind. When we practice mentally, it is easier to perform physically. I find myself doing the same thing before I conduct a teaching seminar. I go over and over my notes during the three-day seminar. During those three days, I am focused only on what I am there to do. I don't let unnecessary distractions get me off course. My staff knows that those days are not good days to tell me about problems unless they have no other choice. I don't want anything fighting for my attention, because I want the words that I speak to be like a laser beam going into the hearts of the listeners.

We each want to be a champion at something. We want to be winners in life. We want to succeed. But sadly, many people don't understand what it takes. They don't discipline their minds, habits, bodies, or finances, and then they wonder why they failed. Discipline is the tool that God gives us to help us be who we say we want to be and do what we say we want to do. Discipline is our friend, not our enemy. Learn to discipline your mind and practice focusing. It may take time and effort, but once you gain a measure of success, you will find life much easier and more fulfilling.

I will admit that focus is more difficult for some people than others. There are actual chemical imbalances that cause problems in this area for some individuals. For those people, too much stimuli or activity is not a good idea. They need to help themselves by creating a space to work in that doesn't hinder their progress. I knew a boy who had attention deficit disorder, and his teacher put him in the front row right in front of her desk, because that was the place he would be the least distracted. I know a teenager who needs to be alone in a room to do homework because she is easily distracted. However, before you claim a chemical disorder and decide that you simply cannot focus well, make sure you are not merely dealing with a lack of mental discipline.

The Sooner, the Better

I find when I have a project that I really need to focus on, the sooner in the day I get started the better it is. If I wait until I have had to deal with too many other things, it can take a mental toll on me. Then I am not as fresh as I would like to be for the project that is my main priority.

It is important that we use our time wisely or we will waste it on things that don't help us do what we need to do. For example, when you are trying to give your attention to a project, someone, or even several people, may ask you a question that *they* feel needs to be answered right away, but in order for you to answer it properly, you have to make three phone calls to get the information you need. Not all of the people you call answer their phone, so you have to keep yours turned on in order to receive their return call, and in the meantime you get more calls and messages. You get five phone calls you were not expecting. Do you have to answer just because they called, or can you decide not to take the call right now and return their call later? Far too often I have decided to take the call and ended up on the phone for thirty minutes with someone who is talking and talking about something that is their priority, but not mine. At times I am headed somewhere and need to stay focused, when I am approached by someone who only needs "one second" of my time. Nobody ever needs one second, so it is best to ask the person to contact you later and stay focused. We cannot avoid all of these situations, but we can learn to manage them better if we truly want to focus on what our priority is.

Try to get to your main priorities while your mind is fresh and not filled with too many other things. Since our thoughts are connected to all of our other feelings and decisions, it is best to keep them peaceful and calm rather than flying in ten different directions. We have only a certain amount of energy for any given day, and if we divide it among too many things, we end up giving a weak effort at best to everything, instead of a focused and creative effort to a few things.

When I woke up this morning, my main goal for the day was to work on my book. I had a goal of finishing a certain number of words by the end of the day if at all possible. I have had some difficulty getting started writing this morning, because I had to deal with about eight other things before I began. Could some of them have been avoided? If I am honest with you and myself, I have to admit they could have. I think one of the most difficult things for us to learn is how to divide what we really must do from the things that we just get caught up in, things we probably should have avoided. But with God's help and some determination, we can do it!

"The sooner the better" is my new catchphrase when it comes to working on my main goals for each day. Any successful person has to develop an ability to choose more important things over less important ones. They are not merely lucky people who don't have interruptions in their life, but they have simply learned to make better choices. Let's decide together to make the best choices every day and choose what is excellent and of the greatest value. Paul prayed this for the churches and I pray it for you...

> ...that you may surely learn to sense what is vital, and approve and prize what is excellent and of real value [recognizing the highest and the best...].
>
> Philippians 1:10

Think About It!

- If you have a goal, something you truly want to accomplish, you will need to focus your thoughts, energies, and time toward it.
- Find out what God has gifted you to do and give yourself wholeheartedly to it.
- In order to stay focused in life, it's important to reprioritize as you go.
- You can't do everything. Choose what is important to you and put your focus on that.
- Discipline is the tool that God gives us to help us be who we say we want to be and do what we say we want to do.

SECTION 2

How Your Thoughts Affect the World Around You

CHAPTER 7

Would You Want to Be Friends with You?

The only way to have a friend is to be one.

Ralph Waldo Emerson

Our thoughts and attitudes affect our friendships in many ways. For example, a positive attitude attracts many friends, whereas someone who is negative may find themselves isolated and alone. Like the old saying goes, "You can catch more flies with honey than vinegar."

I doubt seriously that people who think and speak negatively are aware of how much their negativity affects their relationships with other people. To be honest, the only people who enjoy a negative person are people who are also negative. Anyone who is happy, or wants to be happy, will quickly discover that being with negative, sour people doesn't help them attain or maintain joy. As a matter of fact, they can have a joy-draining effect on others.

I have openly admitted that I spent many years as a very negative person. I have teasingly said that if I thought two positive thoughts in a row my brain would get into a cramp! I can look back and realize that during those years in my life I was lonely and had very few friends. I had no idea why people didn't like me, but I now know that my sour attitude was one of the reasons.

My husband was, and is, very positive, and he has always been a good influence on me in this area. I recall initially getting irritated with him because he was always cheery and hopeful when life seemed so dark and dreary to me. Although he frustrated me at times, I desperately needed and eventually was helped by his positive attitude. The best way to get rid of darkness is to expose it to the light. Dave was a light to me in that his joy eventually made me hungry for a change in my own behavior. One of the best ways we can minister to people is to go out in the world and be a positive, joyful influence on them. If you realize you are a negative-thinking person, the best thing you can do for yourself is to avoid spending excessive time with other negative people and to spend generous amounts of time with positive, hopeful people. Don't accept the lie that you can't be happy because you have too many problems. If anyone can be happy, you can be happy, because God's promises are for anyone who will believe them and receive them by faith.

> *The best way to get rid of darkness is to expose it to the light.*

Do You Attract People to You?

Are you the kind of person whom others want to be friends with? Looking at it in a more personal way, are you the kind of person you would want to be friends with? If I would not even want to be friends with me, how can I expect anyone else to want to? I want to be the kind of person that people are glad to know and call their acquaintance or friend. I want people to be glad they ran into me at Starbucks and we had a few minutes to chat. When

I am at a gathering of people, I would like to be sought out by others because they like my attitude and being with me adds to their joy.

I am sure you feel the same way, but we must also realize that if we want to have that kind of positive effect on people, we need to be positive people. I don't think that anyone would say they don't want people to like them, but they must also realize that nothing good happens accidently. If we want to be well liked, we can choose to be likable. If we want friends, we can choose to be friendly! We have to be kind and do things that make people feel good about themselves when they spend time with us. I once heard that even if people don't remember what you say to them, they do remember how you made them feel.

My exercise coach and trainer is a very enjoyable, positive, encouraging person, and I always look forward to seeing him. His attitude makes the entire experience of working out pleasant. Even though the exercises themselves are usually difficult, he makes me feel like I am amazingly strong through his positive comments to me. He recently told me that I am functioning at about the age of a fifty-year-old woman although I am seventy. I like him a lot!

On the other hand, I had another trainer a few years ago who wasn't very positive or encouraging. When he would correct my form, he would do it in a rather negative, condescending way. He actually thought he was helping me, but the truth was that he was discouraging me. I may have needed the advice, but he could have given it to me in a more encouraging way and perhaps in smaller doses. Excessive correction breaks a person's spirit and makes them weak. He was also very stingy with compliments or praise. Only occasionally did I hear the word "good" come out of his mouth, and even then he didn't say it with much enthusiasm.

It is not hard to realize why I didn't enjoy working with him nearly as much as I do my current trainer.

If anyone has a job dealing with the public or they have clients or customers, it is foolish to be negative and expect to do well.

Give What You Hope to Get

Instead of being focused on me when I am with other people, I need to be focused on them. I have asked God to give me the gift of awareness. I want to train myself to truly be aware of the people around me, their needs, and how I am making them feel. I want to know what they are trying to communicate to me, and that could be different from what they are saying. People who are insecure or in emotional pain are often afraid to reveal their honest needs, so they communicate more vaguely. They hope we will read between the lines, so to speak. They want us to know them and what they need, but they are so fearful of rejection that they will not communicate in a straightforward manner. The only way that we will really "hear" them is if we are listening with our spiritual ears as well as with the ears on our head.

Jesus perceived many things about people that were not obvious to others because He had this gift of awareness. He noticed people that were hurting and He always took time to stop and help them. When we take time to help people, or to genuinely listen to them, it makes them feel valuable.

Jesus noticed a crippled man lying beside a pool of water waiting for a miracle—this man had been there thirty-eight years. Jesus stopped to talk with him and offer help, but I wonder how many others had passed by during those long years, neither noticing the crippled man nor caring to help (see John 5).

Jesus taught us to love our neighbor as we love ourselves, and

He told a story to help us understand what this means. A man had been beaten and robbed and was left to die on the side of the road. Two religious men saw him but passed by on the other side of the street. Have you ever crossed the street, or avoided an aisle in the store, so you could purposely avoid someone with an unpleasant circumstance simply because you didn't want to get involved? More than likely, the answer is yes. One man did stop to help and used his time and money to make sure the man was nursed back to health and Jesus said that he was the only one who truly showed love for the man (see Luke 10:27–36).

If you wouldn't want to be friends with you, then start changing. Give to others what you hope to get. One of the spiritual laws that we are taught in God's Word is that we reap what we sow (see Galatians 6:7). How exciting is that? If we want to gain something, all we need to do is give it to others and it will eventually come back to us. Look at life like a wheel and realize that what you put on the wheel comes back around to you eventually. When we are born again, Jesus gives us a new beginning. Through a relationship with Him, we can learn how to put things on the wheel of life that we actually want to come back to us.

I am not saying that if I am rude to someone one time that it will come back to me. Thankfully, we can apologize and ask for forgiveness and take things off the wheel, but if I continually mistreat other people, it will come back to me. Dave and I have often teased about the wheel principle. If I am just being playful and throw a wet towel at him, he says, "You just put it on the wheel and you know what that means." Before the day is out I can expect a wet towel to be thrown at me! I know how the wheel principle works, and I want to keep it in mind when I am dealing with people in relationships. I want to give them what I want given back to me.

I frequently run into people who are lonely, but after being around them a short period of time I know why. They talk about themselves and their problems incessantly, and their general attitude toward life, work, the government, church, themselves, and other people is all negative and grumpy. They even have a semi-frown on their faces and lots of facial and body language that lets the world know they are dissatisfied individuals. I admit that I don't enjoy being around them, and they don't have a positive influence on me. I don't feel better after being with them, but I do feel drained. These types of negative people are also generous with criticism. Dale Carnegie, author of the well-known book *How to Win Friends and Influence People*, said, "Any fool can criticize, condemn, and complain—and most fools do."[1]

If I don't enjoy being around people who are bitter and critical, why would anyone enjoy being around me if I behave that way? We can learn a lot about how to treat other people by observing how we feel when we are treated badly. I worked at a place for several years where the boss treated most people as inferior to him and insignificant. I knew that God wanted me there during that season of my life, but I honestly didn't understand why He had me placed where I was being mistreated. Many years later, after being in ministry and having several hundred employees, I realized that I had learned a great lesson during those years. I learned how to treat people if I wanted them to respect and like me. I also learned that if we want to please God, we cannot mistreat His children!

Who do you know that makes you feel great when you're with them? Now ask yourself why, and start following their example. I have not always been the best listener in the world. I am great at talking, but not so much at listening. One of the pastors I enjoy being with the most is a great listener. When I talk to him, he acts like every word I say is worth hearing. He never makes me feel rushed or as if he can't wait to get away from me. He rarely interrupts me, because he is more focused on what I am saying than what he wants to say. The lesson is simple: If I want to make others feel the way he makes me feel, then I need to do what he does!

I know a few other people who always make me feel amazing because they encourage and compliment me at least a few times each time I see them. I can follow their example, and I am learning to do so. Choose friends you want to be like, and not people you don't want to be like.

You Become Like the People You Spend Time With

While visiting a prison and spending time with various inmates, a friend shared that most of the inmates connected the beginnings of their lives of crime to being influenced by the wrong group of people. They were not refusing to take responsibility for their crimes, but shared that their troubles started when they joined a gang, or got involved with the wrong man or the wrong woman.

When I was between the ages of eight and twelve, I lived in a neighborhood where most of the children were older than me, and I found that hanging around them led to me doing things I should not have been doing. They influenced me to start smoking cigarettes when I was nine and to frequently lie to my parents about things we were doing. They even convinced me to steal money from my parents and give it to them. It is amazing what we will do to be accepted and feel that we belong. As human beings created for connectedness, we are in danger of making seriously bad decisions in order to avoid being lonely, but then we end up alone anyway, dealing with the problems we created from the bad choices we made.

Just think of the woman who desperately wants to get married and is fearful that her age is getting to be a hindrance. She meets a man who is interested in her, but he is not a Christian like she is, and he has no interest in becoming one. He also has several habits that concern her, like drinking too much and gambling, and he has a quick temper. But in her desperation, she convinces herself that God wants to use her to change him, and in a few months they are married. It doesn't take long for her to realize that she made a serious mistake, but now she is faced with a lifetime of misery and she is still lonely!

Think of the young girl in college who wants to be accepted into a certain sorority and she compromises her moral standards to be accepted by the group. She is excited to be in the group; after all, it is the most prestigious one on campus. But how will she feel when she is expelled from school for underage drinking and drug addiction, neither of which were problems she was even tempted with prior to meeting her "new friends."

Learn to let God be involved in choosing your friends, and you will have ones who make you a better person.

You may not be a negative or a rude person, but if you are around others who are like this for a lengthy period of time, you will start to pick up bad habits. It is like being around people who smoke cigarettes, cigars, or pipes. You may not smoke yourself, but if you're around the smoke, you will end up smelling like smoke anyway.

My daughter-in-law said one time that she knows when my son has stopped by my house with the kids, because they come home smelling like my perfume. This makes me wonder: Do we come home at night smelling like Jesus? Are we positive people with a sweet-smelling fragrance? Second Corinthians 2:14–15 says it this way:

But thanks be to God, Who in Christ always leads us in triumph [as trophies of Christ's victory] and through us spreads and makes evident the fragrance of the knowledge of God everywhere, for we are the sweet fragrance of Christ [which exhales] unto God, [discernible alike] among those who are being saved and among those who are perishing.

Troublemakers

A troublemaker plants seeds of strife; gossip separates the best of friends.

Proverbs 16:28 (NLT)

On several occasions in my close to forty years in ministry, I have had to deal with troublemakers. You may ask, "Joyce, were they Christians?" The answer is yes, but they were Christians who lived more by what they thought and felt instead of by what God's Word teaches. People who are unwise let what they think flow right out of their mouths. For example, when they don't agree with a decision that has been made at work, the first thing they do is make trouble by sowing seeds of strife and gossip. They may cause other people to have a bad opinion regarding something that they should not have gotten involved in to begin with.

It amazes me that when we don't agree with a decision that has been made, we always feel that we are right in our opinions and that those who made the decision are wrong. I often tell people that they don't need to have an opinion in an area where they have no responsibility, and I also still need to remind myself of the same thing at times. Sometimes a restaurant I eat at frequently will take something off the menu that "I" really like, and it irritates me! I have asked why and been told that it was an item that was rarely sold and they were losing money on it. That, of course, had not occurred to me. After all, if "I" like it, surely everyone else does too, so why in the world would they take it off the menu?

Since I am not responsible for the profit of the restaurant, I can have all the opinions I want to about their menu choices, but my opinions are ill informed. It doesn't cost us anything to have an opinion, but if every business followed all of our advice they might go bankrupt. A lot more humility and a lot less pride would do all of us good and would cut down on strife in the world.

Over the years, I have learned how truly dangerous strife is, and I personally avoid the troublemakers who cause it. It is like a poisonous root that spreads quickly and bears bad fruit everywhere it goes. I also aggressively resist letting strife or a root of bitterness get into my own life. I have opportunities to be offended just like anyone else does, but I have learned that I don't have to "take" offense. I can give it right back to Satan, who is the instigator of it.

Recently we dealt with a person who had upset several people at our ministry offices. He had an offense in his heart that had been festering a long time, and although he would have normally been a fairly positive, happy individual, he became negative and was causing strife and division. Thankfully, when confronted, he immediately realized he had let his attitude become poisoned with wrong thinking. He was very repentant and quickly apologized to all the people he had influenced. I would love to be able to say that is what always happens; however, people who allow a root of bitterness to get into their soul are not always that easily persuaded to take responsibility for their bad attitude and make restitution. Sadly, they frequently go from bad to worse until they lose their friends and their jobs.

Beware of Justification

When you are offended and participating in strife, it is wise to examine your thoughts. If you find that you are justifying having a bad attitude, I encourage you to realize that justifying any bad behavior that the Word of God condemns is a dangerous thing. It keeps us deceived and unable to take ownership of our faults. Nobody enjoys saying, "I was wrong—please forgive me," but it is one of the most powerful six-word sentences in the world. It brings peace to turmoil; joy replaces frustration and misery and puts a smile on God's face. He is delighted when we follow His ways instead of our own carnal thoughts, feelings, and behaviors.

God has changed me dramatically over the course of my life and ministry, and I expect that He will continue doing so. But in every instance, I have been required to face a truth about myself that ended up making me free. If we continue in His Word, we will know the truth and the truth will make us free (see John 8:31–32). Self-justification is dangerous because it prevents us from seeing what God wants us to see in order for things to be better in our lives.

When I attempt to justify myself, I always find an excuse for my bad behavior. I know the behavior is wrong, and I would more than likely condemn it in someone else, but I have given myself a free pass. The apostle Paul said that we judge others for what we do (see Romans 2:1). The only way that is possible is if we justify our behavior in our own thinking by finding an excuse for why we do it. We excuse ourselves, but for others, we may think there is no excuse! For example, I might think there is no excuse for Dave to be irritable with me, and I tell him so fervently. But if I am irritable with him and he confronts me, I might excuse myself by saying that I don't feel well or that I have had a rough day. If we would be as merciful with others as we are with ourselves, I am sure that everyone would feel more loved.

> *If you want friends, be the kind of person that other people want to be around.*

The message in this chapter is very simple: If you want friends, be the kind of person that other people want to be around. If you realize that you are rather negative or that you have let the disappointments of life sour your attitude, ask God to start changing you. Facing truth is the doorway to freedom!

Think about this: Do you have friends who help you be a better person, and are you the kind of person you would want to be friends with, or would you stay away from someone like you? How can you be a better friend? Are you the source of strife in any situation? If you need to make a change, then make a change quickly. Thank God we can always change! Facing truth and changing accordingly is what a wise person does. A foolish one avoids truth and justifies his behavior even though God has judged it in His Word.

Think About It!

- Negative people have a negative, joy-draining effect on others.
- Give away what you hope to receive—hope, encouragement, joy, and laughter.
- Look at life like a wheel and realize that what you put on the wheel comes back around to you eventually.
- Be the kind of person that others want to be around.

CHAPTER 8

Positive Self-Talk

For as he thinks in his heart, so is he.

Proverbs 23:7

I can say without hesitation that learning the power of thoughts and how they are connected to every other area of my life was, and still is, amazing to me. They not only affect how we talk to others, but also how we talk to ourselves. And maintaining proper self-talk affects us in every aspect of our lives.

It is God's will that you love yourself in a healthy, balanced way. If you dislike and disrespect yourself, your self-talk will be negative and devastating to your spiritual growth and progress in spiritual maturity. We don't need to be in love with ourselves or be the center of our universe, but we must maintain a healthy self-image. This is only possible by knowing the love of God personally, as well as His grace, forgiveness, mercy, and long-suffering kindness. We can love ourselves because God loves us! We may not, and probably should not, love everything we do, because we all sin and come short of God's perfect standard. But we can love the person God has created us to be, the one we are always in the process of becoming through Christ.

How we talk to ourselves about ourselves is vitally important to our own self-image as well as to how we relate to other people. We all talk to ourselves about ourselves, but some people have never learned just how much their own thoughts influence how they feel about themselves and how important it is to every other area of their lives. Do you like yourself? One of the most important things I have learned during my journey with God is that I cannot have good relationships with anyone else if I don't have a good relationship with myself. Here, we plainly see the mind connection. My thoughts about me are connected to my thoughts and attitudes toward others.

If I am harsh, hard and legalistic, critical and condemning with myself, then I will be the same way with other people. Some people expect more of themselves than they can possibly achieve and, by doing so, they put terrible pressure on themselves. If we do that to ourselves, we will usually do the same thing to other people.

A mother who is a perfectionist will not only expect perfection from herself, but also she will expect and demand it from her children. A young mother who has perfectionist tendencies told me this story:

> One day while on vacation with my family, I had to apologize to them because I had a grouchy attitude toward them. After the apology, I took some time to ask God why I was behaving that way with them when in reality they had not done anything deserving of the type of behavior I displayed. He showed me that I was having guilty thoughts that morning about myself because I tend to be slower to do things than other people. I have been that way all of my life and suffered a lot with guilt because of it. I have times when I realize that I don't have to be like anyone else, and I am able to accept myself as a child of God who is loved by Him, but on that day I had fallen

back into bad habits. The way I was thinking and feeling about myself came out of me in a wrong behavior toward my family.

If we take the time to do it, we can almost always connect wrong behavior to some type of wrong thinking.

> *We can almost always connect wrong behavior to some type of wrong thinking.*

Receiving Mercy

What types of things do you think when your behavior is less than perfect? If you make a mistake, are your thoughts, *I am not what I should be; I am a bad person*? Or do you think, *I am sorry I made a mistake, but I am grateful for God's mercy that is new every morning*?

God doesn't want us to live under the tyranny of unrealistic expectations. He does not want us to be pressured, but He desires that we receive mercy for our failures. As human beings, we will make mistakes and probably make them every day. Jesus came for those who are needy, imperfect, and weak. He came to help, to rescue, to deliver, and to save.

If we could manifest perfection, we would not need a savior. We do have weaknesses, but we do not need to hate ourselves because of them. We should give other people who are imperfect the same mercy that God gives us. Don't reject people because they don't meet an unrealistic standard that you have set for them.

It is widely known today that many people have eating disorders, self-mutilation problems, and addictions of all types, and they even attempt suicide because they feel that the pressure of other people's expectations is just too much. Perhaps their parents or teachers are never quite satisfied with their grades in school, or their performance in sports, or how they keep their rooms, or their personal appearance. Let's be merciful with others, and ourselves, in the same way that God is merciful and long-suffering with us.

> And if you had only known what this saying means, I desire mercy [readiness to help, to spare, to forgive] rather than sacrifice and sacrificial victims, you would not have condemned the guiltless.
>
> Matthew 12:7

How can we determine if we are too hard on ourselves or other people? It is quite simple. How often do we become upset with ourselves, and ultimately other people, because our performance is less than stellar? Do you demand sacrifices from yourself or others as payment for past mistakes? I spent years sacrificing my joy to pay for my mistakes. I can safely say that I was mad at myself most of the time for something I felt I was doing or wasn't doing. I thought I had no right to enjoy life because of my faults, but thankfully, I finally learned that Jesus offers me good things I don't deserve, and I don't have to pay for my sins because He has satisfied the debt I owed through offering Himself. When I stopped trying to make myself pay for my mistakes, I found it much easier to stop trying to make others pay for their mistakes.

I spent most of the first twenty years of my marriage to Dave upset about something that either he or the children weren't doing. When I realized how bad my behavior was toward them, I wanted to change, but I couldn't until I figured out I was typically upset with myself as well. We can give to others only what we have inside of us. How I think of myself is how I will think of others, and the attitude I have toward myself is what I will pass along to my family and friends. If I don't know how to receive forgiveness and mercy, I won't give it to other people, and if I pressure myself to perform perfectly, I will do the same thing to people I associate with.

Anyone can immediately relieve pressure from their lives by deciding to take a different attitude toward their own weaknesses and faults, as well as those of other people.

When I finally did learn to be more merciful with myself and other people, it did relieve a lot of pressure and frustration in my life. Going through life demanding something that is impossible to ever have is a setup for never-ending misery.

It took me many years to learn to receive God's mercy simply because I was never given any while I was a child, but once I began to recognize and receive the mercy of God, I became a much happier person. My relationships improved because people want to be in a relationship with those who love and accept them without pressuring them to be something they don't know how to be.

There are several reasons why people find it difficult to receive mercy. I've listed a few of them below. See if any of these have affected your life.

1. They were not given any mercy as a child.
2. They have perfectionist temperaments and usually see what is wrong instead of what is right.
3. They may have learned improper teaching about God's character. (Note: God is not mad at you! However, if you have a rule-oriented, religious attitude, you will think that God is expecting things from you that He isn't, and you'll end up pressured continually by fear that He is angry or displeased.)

4. They feel mercy is not fair. It is given to those who don't deserve it, and that is very difficult for some people to grasp.

If you recognize any of these "mercy stoppers" in your life, you can ask God to help you overcome them so you can receive the mercy He so freely gives. When you begin to think right about the mercy of God in your life, it will change the way you see yourself. For example, let's look at the last item in our list...

It wasn't fair for Jesus to take our sin upon Him and be punished for what others had done wrong, but He did it. Life isn't fair, but God is just, and there is a huge difference between the two. Life may not treat everyone fairly, but you can trust that God will always bring justice. He will reward us for everything we do that is done in obedience to Him, even if we don't understand why He is asking us to do it.

It didn't seem fair for God to require me to totally forgive my father, who sexually abused me, and even go to the extreme of taking care of him in his old age, but God has blessed me greatly for doing so. When I realized how much God forgives me every day, I realized His abundant mercy toward me; in turn, I was able to show mercy and forgiveness to my father. It will be much easier for you to be merciful with others once you are fully aware of how much mercy God offers to you. Mercy cannot be earned, or otherwise it would not be mercy. Mercy can be received only with gratitude! I recommend spending a few minutes every day in thought about how merciful God is to you, and then plan to be merciful to others as you go through your day.

> It will be much easier for you to be merciful with others once you are fully aware of how much mercy God offers to you.

We can prepare ourselves for right action through practicing right thinking on purpose.

Be Nicer to Yourself

Are you kind to yourself? Do you say nice things to you about yourself, or are you more inclined to meditate on all of your faults? If we want to walk with God, we need to learn to think like God thinks. What does God think of you? He thinks you are awesome and that you have great possibilities. He is not blind to our faults, but He looks at them in light of our entire life and not just one event in which we didn't behave well. If you love God, that is the most important thing to Him, and love covers a multitude of sins (see 1 Peter 4:8). Don't focus on all your faults, because God doesn't. I can assure you that there is more right with you than there is wrong, but perhaps you have never taken the time to see it.

Here are some things that God says about you in His Word:

You are a new creature in Christ, old things have passed away and all things are made new.

2 Corinthians 5:17

Jesus became sin for you and has made you the righteousness of God in Him.

2 Corinthians 5:21

He has handpicked you. He has chosen you to be His own in Christ because He loves you.

Ephesians 1:4–5

You have the mind of Christ, the ability to think as He thinks.

1 Corinthians 2:16

You have gifts, talents, and abilities.

Romans 12:5–6

God has a good plan for your future.

Jeremiah 29:11

God has accepted you and He will never reject you.

Ephesians 2:6

You are completely forgiven and God has forgotten your sins.

Hebrews 10:17

You are the home of God.

1 Corinthians 3:16

God created you and everything He created is good.

Genesis 1:31

God calls us His friend.

John 15:15

We are called God's beloved.

Romans 9:25

It seems that it is more natural for us to think about what is wrong with us instead of what is right with us. As believers in Jesus Christ, we are frequently warned in Scripture about the dangers of pride, which is thinking that we are more important, or better, than other people. However, we can realize that we are important to God and His overall plan for mankind without thinking we are better than other people. We are new creatures in Him, and we need to think of ourselves accordingly.

Even recently God reminded me to believe that it is His will for me to think good things about myself instead of merely seeing my faults. I never want to ignore my faults, or not take ownership of and responsibility for them. But at the same time, if that is all I think of, I will become negative and discouraged about myself, and my improper self-talk and self-image will reflect on all my other relationships. God views us as being right with Him through Jesus Christ. He sees us and thinks of us as being in Christ, and we should learn to do the same thing. In ourselves,

> *God views us as being right with Him through Jesus Christ.*

we are nothing of any value, and we can do very little right, but "in Christ," we are amazing people who have been re-created in Christ Jesus. We are born anew that we may do the good works that He has prearranged and made ready for us, that we may live the good life Jesus died for us to have (see Ephesians 2:10). God wants us to see ourselves the way He does! He wants us to have a good life!

God has provided a good life for us, but our minds and attitudes must be completely renewed if we want to actually see it in our daily lives. One of the most important verses of Scripture for us to understand regarding our thoughts is Romans 12:2:

> *Do not be conformed to this world (this age), [fashioned after and adapted to its external, superficial customs], but be transformed (changed) by the [entire] renewal of your mind [by its new ideals and its new attitude], so that you may*

prove [for yourselves] what is the good and acceptable and
perfect will of God, even the thing which is good and accept-
able and perfect [in His sight for you].

I was a Christian for at least twenty years before I ever even
heard this Scripture or had any idea that my thoughts mattered
at all. I certainly had no idea that I had a choice about what I
thought and that my mind was indeed connected to my words,
attitudes, and behavior. I think I can say that my relationship
with God never moved beyond a kindergarten level until I understood the power of thoughts and words. Perhaps this is new to
you too, and if it is, then you are embarking on a new beginning
that will be truly amazing as you follow through. I know for me,
the understanding of the mind connection was one of the biggest
breakthroughs in my spiritual life.

Developing a good relationship with yourself will help you in
many ways. You spend every moment of your life with "you,"
so it stands to reason that if you don't like you, then you will be
unhappy. With God's help, not only can you think better thoughts
about yourself, but you can also take the time to do things for
yourself that you enjoy. God wants us to help others and be available for a wide variety of good works that He has planned; however, if you never take the time to do anything for yourself, you
will quickly become burned out from always giving and never
receiving. You will begin to feel like people take advantage of you,
but that wrong attitude can be avoided by simply taking time to
do things that you enjoy, along with doing things for other people.

We often wait for other people to do things for us and it's nice
when they do, but even if they don't, we can still do things for
ourselves in order to maintain a balanced, healthy emotional life.
When you feel worn out and taken advantage of, you can go to

Jesus for advice and you may hear Him say, "Take the day off and do something you enjoy."

If you treat yourself better in your thoughts and your actions, I can assure you that you will begin to treat others better also. What goes on *in* us is what comes *out* of us, in words, attitudes, and behaviors. Instead of just being irritated because your life is out of balance, do something to change it. It is your life, and God expects you to manage it wisely!

Think About It!

- The way we talk to and think about ourselves affects us in every area of our lives.
- It is God's will for you to love yourself in a healthy, balanced way.
- When you stop trying to make yourself pay for your mistakes, it is much easier to stop trying to make others pay for theirs.
- It will be much easier for you to be merciful with others once you are fully aware of how much mercy God offers to you.
- God loves you. He thinks you are wonderful, and He has filled your life with great possibilities.
- God doesn't focus on your faults; why should you?

CHAPTER 9

Thoughtless Actions

To build may have to be the slow and laborious task of years. To destroy can be the thoughtless act of a single day.
Winston Churchill

We do many things without thinking and that is, perhaps, one of the most dangerous things we can do. Thoughtless acts bring mental and emotional pain, and deterioration and destruction to relationships as well as many other areas. People say thoughtless things to others, causing pain and perhaps ruining their day. We do things without thinking, like saying things at inappropriate times, making impulsive purchases, making various commitments without seriously considering whether or not we can complete them. We quite often practice what I call "mindless eating," eating without being fully aware that we are doing it. We stop to talk with a coworker who has a dish of candy on her desk, and while we are talking, we mindlessly eat three pieces of chocolate candy. We walk past a dish of cookies on a table in a furniture store of all places (this happened to me) and without thinking we take one and eat it while we are shopping!

We have many "thoughtless actions," but this book is about learning to not only think, but also to do so purposely and correctly.

How often do you need to apologize to someone, and say something like this: "I am sorry I hurt you—I just wasn't thinking." Our lives would be so much better if we did form a habit of thinking before speaking or taking action. I imagine it will take a lifetime of continued discipline to ever accomplish it completely, but at least we can start moving in the right direction.

In his book *The Spiritual Man*, Watchman Nee said a lot about the dangers of a passive mind. It was from his teaching that I first began to realize that we could do our own thinking instead of just passively meditating on whatever happens to fall into our minds. Some thoughts are not necessarily good or evil; they are merely useless! We will call them gray thoughts. They come from something we noticed, or recalled, or perhaps we can find no source for them at all. There are also what I will refer to as bright thoughts and dark thoughts. The dark ones are thoughts that do damage—they are very destructive and usually negative. Thankfully, there are good thoughts that let the light into our minds and give us good feelings and positive energy.

For example, if I am riding down the highway in a car and I think, *There sure are lots of birds sitting on that electric power line*, that is just a gray thought about something I observed. However, if I am riding down the road and I think, *There is no way that God could love me after all the things I have done wrong*, that is a dark lie injected into my mind by the devil, who is hoping to prevent me from ever receiving God's love and forgiveness. If I am riding in the same car, on the same road, and I think, *Good things are going to happen to me and through me today. God loves me and gives me His favor all day long*, that is a holy, pure, good thought that lets light into my soul.

Try to always find the good, bright thoughts!

The Battlefield of the Mind

Many Christians today don't want to hear anything about the devil. They think it's an unpleasant topic of conversation, but thinking like that will open the door for deception and error. The devil is alive and active on planet Earth, and we may as well be aware of him and learn how to deal with him aggressively. The basic truth is that the devil is a liar, and he uses our mind as a battlefield to do warfare with us. He is the source of dark and harmful thoughts. His goal is to prevent us from enjoying the good plan that God has for us, and he is successful if we never learn to recognize how he attacks our minds. Scripture teaches us that our mind is a battleground where a war is being fought.

> For though we walk (live) in the flesh, we are not carrying on our warfare according to the flesh and using mere human weapons.
>
> For the weapons of our warfare are not physical [weapons of flesh and blood], but they are mighty before God for the overthrow and destruction of strongholds, [inasmuch as we] refute arguments and theories and reasonings and every proud and lofty thing that sets itself up against the [true] knowledge of God; and we lead every thought and purpose away captive into the obedience of Christ (the Messiah, the Anointed One).
>
> 2 Corinthians 10:3–5

We see from these verses that we are definitely in a war and that it has to do with our thought realm. This war is a spiritual war! Thoughts cannot be seen, but we do see the results of them. Thoughts operate in the spiritual realm, and, perhaps for this reason, we fail to realize just how powerful they are.

> Thoughts cannot be seen, but we do see the results of them.

We tend to ignore what we cannot see with our eyes, and yet God's Word teaches as much about the unseen spiritual realm as it does the seen natural realm.

The Scriptures in 2 Corinthians don't outright say that the devil puts these thoughts in our minds, but everything evil comes from him. So it stands to reason that if the thoughts are destructive, or they are ones that are going to hinder us or steal God's best for us, they were initiated by the devil. And there are other Scriptures we should consider that tell us plainly that Satan instigates evil thoughts.

The apostle John wrote that Satan had put the thought of betraying Jesus into the heart of Judas (see John 13:2). Ananias and his wife, Sapphira, sold a piece of property with the intention and commitment to give the money to help the destitute and poor, but they deceptively kept part of the money for themselves. Acts 5:3 says, "But Peter said, Ananias, why has Satan filled your heart that you should lie to and attempt to deceive the Holy Spirit, and should [in violation of your promise] withdraw secretly and appropriate to your own use part of the price from the sale of the land?"

In my opinion, it would do every Christian a lot of good to do a thorough and well-informed study of Scripture concerning our enemy the devil and how he works. We never need to fear him, for God has given us power and authority to deal with him, but we must not be ignorant of his wiles. Paul wrote to the Corinthians and instructed them to forgive in order to keep Satan from getting the advantage over them, and he went on to say they were not to be ignorant of his wiles and intentions (see 2 Corinthians 2:10–11). He wanted them to be informed about how Satan operated and what to do in order to not be deceived by him.

I was a Christian for many years before I was taught anything about the devil or the fact that he attacks people in the realm of their thoughts. When I did begin to learn, the knowledge did not frighten me; it empowered me to take ownership of my thoughts and learn how to recognize where my thoughts were coming from and whether to accept or reject them.

One day, I was talking with a young man who is an active member of a large, well-known denomination. We were discussing several things about God's Word and missions, and enjoying the conversation. But when I mentioned something about the devil trying to prevent us from doing something while on a mission field, the young man went totally silent, and I could tell that talking about the devil made him uncomfortable. I couldn't help thinking how much it would add to his life and walk with God if he truly knew who his enemy was and how to resist him.

Some preachers and Bible teachers say nothing or very little about things like the devil, demons, and spiritual warfare. They often say, "I would rather preach on the light than the darkness." Actually, I agree that is normally the best plan, but as teachers of God's Word, we are responsible to produce well-informed believers who know how to recognize when the devil is at work, and how to resist him.

What Have You Been Thinking About?

Instead of being "unthinking" people, we can train ourselves to think about what we are thinking about. If your mood begins to sink, or an attitude is ungodly, take an inventory of your current thoughts and you will very likely find the culprit. I enjoy knowing that I can do something about my prob-

> We can train ourselves to think about what we are thinking about.

lems, and I hope that you do also. It is exciting to me to realize that I don't have to sit passively by and let the devil fill my mind with poisonous and destructive thoughts, but I can learn to recognize them, and by a simple act of my will, I can think about something else that will be beneficial.

This morning I spent some time looking over my calendar for the next three weeks. I saw all the commitments I had, and I discussed them with Dave. Shortly after that, I felt pressured and mildly irritated. When I stopped to think about what I was thinking about, I realized that I was looking at all I had to do in one huge lump instead of trusting God to give me His strength and ability one day at a time. God gives us grace (His power and ability) daily to do the things we need to do if we trust Him, but He doesn't give us grace to put in the bank, so to speak. When we worry about things that haven't taken place yet, we are on our own. God doesn't help us with those things, because His will is that we fully live and enjoy today, while trusting Him completely for the future.

Worrying, Wondering, and Wandering

When we worry, we let our minds wander around from the past to the present to the future, and we wonder or reason about what is going to happen to us, and we lose our peace. God intends for us to keep our minds on what we are doing. I don't mean to say that we never take time to learn from the past or to make plans for the future. But when we do, it should be something we do purposely, and not the result of a wild mind that never focuses on anything. All these types of thoughts will pressure us, because they are not God's will. The prophet Isaiah said that God would keep us in perfect peace when our mind is fixed on Him.

> *You will guard him and keep him in perfect and constant peace whose mind [both its inclination and its character] is stayed on You, because he commits himself to You, leans on You, and hopes confidently in You.*
>
> Isaiah 26:3

The writer of Proverbs stated that the good man would be satisfied with "[the fruit of] his ways [with the holy thoughts and actions which his heart prompts and in which he delights]" (Proverbs 14:14).

Do you want to be peaceful, guarded by God, and satisfied? Then you need to realize that it begins with the thoughts that you choose to think. Your mind is connected to every feeling you have and every action that you take.

If you give yourself over to worry and reasoning, your thoughts may sound like this: *How am I going to do everything I have to do? My life is impossible! This is more than I can handle.* Instead of worrying about the future, you could think things like: *God loves me, and He will take care of everything in my future. He will give me the strength and ability to do each thing I need to do as it comes up.* I am not merely making suggestions for you to follow, but I actually do what I am advising you to do.

Right at this particular time in my life, I am dealing with a physical issue that is not serious, but it is irritating. After six weeks of doctors and various medicines, it is still not completely gone. My thoughts want to wander and wonder, and when I allow them to do so, this is how they sound: *What if this never goes away? This is putting pressure on me and making everything else I have to do more difficult. I don't know what to do. I am frustrated.* However, when I choose my own thoughts according to God's promises, this is how they sound: *This is uncomfortable, but there are millions of people right now in much worse situations than this. This will pass. God will provide an answer. My health issue is not completely gone, but it is much better than it was two weeks ago. I believe that God's healing power is working in me right now, and I am getting better and better all the time.*

"Unthinking" thoughts never go in a direction that will help us. They are useless at best and tormenting at worst. When you begin making an effort to do your own thinking, you may well feel that you will never accomplish it. It might be likened to deciding to tame a wild animal. It will take time, patience, and help from God, which you receive through asking for it and leaning on Him at all times. Learning to choose your own thoughts also requires the wisdom to not condemn yourself when you are not successful. Guilt and condemnation steal your energy and they accomplish nothing. They keep you going around and around the same mountain, so to speak. However, the person who is determined and patient will inherit the promises of God.

> *For you have need of steadfast patience and endurance, so that you may perform and fully accomplish the will of God, and thus receive and carry away [and enjoy to the full] what is promised.*
> Hebrews 10:36

Be Thoughtful

Since our thoughts do affect the way we relate to people and the world around us, it's helpful to learn to "be thoughtful." Take time to think through your day before you begin it. Of course we don't know everything a day will hold, but we all hopefully have some plan. Being thoughtful about your day on purpose is very different from worrying about it. I will use my day today as an example. I plan to write until around 1 p.m. During that time, I need quiet so I am purposely going to not get involved in other things. At 1 p.m. I am going to get dressed and do my hair and makeup and go to an appointment that I have.

I am following my own advice to do some things I enjoy in the midst of my work. I plan to be friendly with and compliment the people I come in contact with. Anytime we are out in public, we should see it as an opportunity to represent Jesus to other people. It is wise to be thoughtful, because everyone we meet is probably fighting some kind of battle. Smile at everyone, because it is a sign of acceptance, and remember that a smile is the most beautiful thing you can wear.

When I go out today, instead of merely being self-aware, I plan to be aware of other people and their needs. After my appointment, I am meeting with Dave, and I will ask him about his day and listen patiently as he tells me about his golf swing and the new thing he learned that he is sure will be "the thing" that will be the answer he has been looking for (he has been looking for forty years and has a new thing two or three times a month :)). We are going to meet two other couples for dinner. This is also an opportunity to be a blessing to them. I want to be thoughtful and interested in what they are doing in ministry instead of taking up the evening talking about myself and what I am doing.

When I am with people, I plan to make them feel important, and one of the ways I can do that is to show genuine interest in them. Earlier this morning, I found myself thinking that we would split the bill. But then I decided to do my own thinking, and I thought about the Scripture that says it is more blessed to give than to receive, so I decided we would pay for dinner, because that is another way we can be thoughtful of others.

Being thoughtful about the parts of my day I know about helps me behave the way that pleases God instead of just reacting to things out of unthinking habits. Things will happen today that I am not planning, but I intend to respond calmly to those things I had not planned. Hopefully, you can see that being thoughtful about people and events will help you in many ways.

We all want friends that are thoughtful, and the best way to have them is to be to others what we want them to be to us. I have some friends that I can truthfully say are very thoughtful people, and others who are not. We can learn to be more thoughtful by observing people who are.

This morning I received a short three-minute video by e-mail from a couple we financially support who have a wonderful ministry in Russia. They told us they pray for us before they even get out of bed in the morning, and they spoke over and over of how they appreciate our partnership with them. I was encouraged, to say the least. The man said that although he prays for us each morning, this morning when he prayed, he had the idea to go to his recording studio and make the video. How thoughtful! He had to leave his home and travel to his studio in order to record a three-minute video just for the sole purpose of encouraging me. I believe God gives all of us good ideas of ways we can bless others, but we may not hang on to the thought long enough to take action.

When good things come into your mind, keep them and ask

God if you need to take action on them. When bad things come into your mind, reject them as soon as you recognize them, because they are not going to help you or anyone else. When you have a thought about being a blessing to someone else, and that good thought is followed immediately by a bad thought discouraging you from doing the good thing, realize that the second thought is a product of the devil trying to stop you. Let's be committed to choosing the good and resisting the evil continually, just as God instructs us in His Word (see Deuteronomy 30:19).

The best way to resist thoughtless actions that always hurt us or other people is to fill our day with being thoughtful on purpose! Mark Twain reportedly said, "Kindness is the language which the deaf can hear and the blind can see."[1]

I encourage you to start "Operation Nice," and do things like letting someone else go in front of you in line at the grocery store, saying "please" and "thank you" all day, telling people you appreciate them, cleaning up after yourself instead of leaving a mess for someone else, and being kinder than you feel like being.

Think About It!

- Our lives would be so much better if we formed a habit of thinking before speaking or taking action.
- Scripture teaches us that our mind is a battleground where a war is being fought.
- Instead of being "unthinking," you can train yourself to think about what you are thinking about.
- Be intentional in your thinking—take the time to think through your day before you begin it.

CHAPTER 10

The Power of Perspective

I don't think of all the misery, but of the beauty that still remains.

Anne Frank

Books have been written and movies have been produced about Anne Frank. These works always bring out how great her perspective was in the midst of the atrocities of the Holocaust. This didn't happen because she was a pessimist and focused on everything that was wrong in her life, but because she had a rare ability to see beauty in the midst of horrifying events. I think most people reading her story would say, "I wish I was like that." We will not become that way by wishing, but by purposely deciding how we will view life.

Each of us has a perspective on life. We see things and think about things in a specific way. Some are very quick to see all the problems and magnify them, while others have made a choice to minimize the impact of difficulty by looking for the beauty, the good in life and in people. On a scale of one to ten, where would you put yourself when it comes to your overall thinking? Ten would be perfect, and one would be slightly better than zero. I think I might be at about a seven, and on some days an eight. I still have a lot of growing to do, but if I keep a good perspective, I can be happy about the fact that I am no longer a one on the scale like I once was. Lots of years have passed since God began teaching me the power of my thoughts and how to think purposely instead of passively. And I am very glad to have the experience that I now have so I can share passionately with you what I've learned about the mind connection.

Born Lucky?

Was Anne Frank just an optimistic girl who happened to be born with a great outlook on life? She may have had a few "happy genes" that not all of us have, but she still had to make choices and decisions about how she was going to think and what she was going to say. Far too many people passively wait for something good to come their way, when they should be aggressively choosing to do what is right, including learning to think right.

There is a fable told of a father from a wealthy family who took his son out to the country in order to show him how poor people live. This father and son spent several days on a farm with a family most people would consider extremely poor.

After the trip, when the father asked the son what he had observed, the son replied, "I saw how blessed that family is! We have a pool in our garden, but they have a creek with no end. We have imported lanterns, and they have the stars at night. We buy our food, but they grow theirs." The dad was speechless as his son remarked, "Thanks, Dad, for showing me how poor we are."[1]

Perspective is a wonderful thing. The father in this story saw only what the poor people didn't have, but the son saw what they did have. The boy, upon seeing it through a different lens, obviously ended up feeling his family was poorer than the people they went to learn from.

The young man in this story was assured of having an amazing life that was not based on his circumstances. Anyone who learns to see life the way he did, who can find the good in everything, cannot be defeated by circumstances.

In our American culture today, I wonder how many millions of times each day someone thinks, *The world is a mess!* I hear it all the time, and you probably do too. They lower their head a bit, then shake it slowly back and forth in dismay, and say with either an angry or a depressed voice, "The world is a mess!" It never makes me feel better to hear it, how about you? To be honest, I get weary of the same old attitude and dreary outlook. You might be thinking, *Well, Joyce, the world* is *a mess!* While it is true that we do have problems, I cannot give up the belief that good things are happening also, and I would personally like to hear more about them.

Sin abounds these days, and when that is the case, circumstances are never good. However, talking incessantly about the problems in the world today won't get rid of them. I am not implying that we should ignore the violence and sit idly by and do nothing but sing happy tunes and smile. We need to pray, we need to be informed, and we need to take God-inspired action to see things turn around for the better. But we don't need to rehearse over and over how bad things are and behave as if God is incapable of changing things.

When circumstances are bad in any society or anyone's personal life, focusing on them and saying negative things about already negative situations doesn't increase our personal joy or anyone else's. People need hope, and we can make the choice to be committed to giving it to them. The next time someone tells you how bad things are in the world, say something like this: "Yes, things sure are bad, but I do believe that God has a plan for His people." Anyone I have said that to always responds, "Yes,

> *People need hope, and we can make the choice to be committed to giving it to them.*

you are right." They just needed to be reminded of something that had gotten pushed into the background of their mind because of the massive amounts of negative input coming at them.

Put On God's Glasses

Jesus teaches us by word and example to be positive about the problems of life, and so do the apostles. Jesus said that in the world we would have tribulation but that we should cheer up because He has overcome the world (see John 16:33). Awesome! Keep that in mind when life seems bleak. When the disciples were in a severe storm and Jesus was asleep in the bottom of the boat, they became very frightened and were focused only on the storm. But Jesus rebuked them for their lack of faith, and He asked them why they were upset since He was with them (see Mark 4:36–40). Jesus wanted them to see Him as greater than the storm.

Apparently Anne Frank saw God when others saw only persecution. She must have been looking through God's glasses. The Lord sees things differently than we often do. We see problems, but He sees possibilities. We see messes, but He sees miracles. We see endings, but He sees new beginnings. We see pain and pressure, but He sees spiritual growth.

You might wonder, *Doesn't God care about all the horrible problems in the world?* Yes, He certainly does, and let me assure you that God does have a good plan for not only society in general, but also for each of us individually. Hang on to that biblical truth, and don't let anything going on in the world take it from you.

I am in the midst of studying the book of Exodus, and I noticed that when all the terrible plagues were being unleashed on Egypt due to Pharaoh's disobedience, God's people were kept safe. Exodus says that when God sent a swarm of something called "bloodsucking gadflies" (and I am happy we don't have those around these days, unless they have just been renamed "mosquitoes"), He set apart the land of Goshen for the Israelites, which had no swarms of gadflies (see Exodus 8:21–22). No matter how many bloodsucking gadflies you run into every day, they don't have to be a problem for you!

And when all the livestock were killed, God made a distinction between the livestock of Israel and the livestock of Egypt. He then declared that nothing belonging to the Israelites would die (see Exodus 9:4). When Egypt was plummeted with weighty hail, only in the land of Goshen, where the Israelites were, was there no hail (see Exodus 9:26).

And when it was so dark in the land of Egypt that the people could not even see well enough to get out of bed for three days, all the Israelites had natural light (see Exodus 10:23).

I do realize that people reading this, or other people you might know, have suffered property loss due to floods, hurricanes, or fires, and it would be easy to say, "Wait a minute, God didn't take care of them." My point is that even though Anne Frank and many others like her throughout history endured much suffering, their perspective allowed them to have joy in the midst of the agony. Our attitudes can make our problems harder to deal with or easier—it is up to us.

> *Our attitudes can make our problems harder to deal with or easier—it is up to us.*

I've seen this up close and personal. Our ministry has been heavily involved in disaster relief, and I have seen individuals who become bitter and blame God, but I have also seen others who always find something they believe God spared them from or is doing for them. I don't even need to tell you which of these two types of people were happier.

I think Anne Frank made a choice for herself. She couldn't do anything about her situation, but she could control her attitude, and by doing so, she became someone whom God could use as an example to the world. Just think about it—although it has been about seventy years since she died, Anne Frank is still well known today. I have not read a book about anyone from that time period heralding their negative, hopeless, bitter attitude, have you?

I find these things to be *very* encouraging, and they give me hope concerning the things I see taking place in the world today. Let me say firmly that *God has a plan for his people*, and we should think, speak, and behave as if we believe that He does. Let's learn to see through the glasses that God looks through! Let's learn to have His perspective!

The Long-Range Effect of Perspective

Since our perspective involves our thought processes, we would be wise to realize that it also affects our moods. If I am in a bad mood, I may need a perspective adjustment. Perhaps I am looking too much at what I don't have and not enough at what I do have. Or I may be looking at what people don't do for me, instead of what they do for me. Our perspective on anything, especially events and people we don't like, have a long-range effect. How we view events that took place as far back as our childhood may still be affecting us in a negative manner.

When I learned to think of the abuse in my childhood as something that was unfortunate, but something that could be used by God for good, the pain began to lessen and I began to heal emotionally. As long as I deeply resented my father for sexually abusing me and my mother for not protecting me, I had a wound in my soul that could not heal. But when I decided to try to understand the way my father was raised, and my mother's fear and weakness of character, I actually started feeling more sorry for them than I did for myself.

If you are dealing with a broken heart or a wounded soul, try asking God to help you make a connection between your perspective and your current feelings. If you are willing to change the way you view the situation (and it is not always easy), you will begin to make progress toward wholeness instead of remaining broken. Life breaks all of us in one way or another, and it is up to us whether we remain broken and bitter or we let God use it to make us better and more powerful.

> If you are willing to change the way you view the situation (and it is not always easy), you will begin to make progress toward wholeness instead of remaining broken.

Let me take a moment to say that I fully understand that it is much easier for me to write about looking at painful things in a positive way than it is to do it. However, it is possible and is, in fact, the only choice we have unless we want to remain miserable. Although opening up old wounds for the purpose of having them cleansed is painful, it is more painful to remain wounded and broken all of our lives. We cannot do anything about the past, but we can do a great deal about the future. I encourage you not to remain stuck in a painful place when God is offering you healing. It is never too late for a new beginning.

Perspective and Power

I believe that Anne Frank was empowered by her perspective on her circumstances. It enabled her to remain hopeful, which is vital in difficult times. God's Word states that "hope deferred makes the heart sick" (Proverbs 13:12). When we are hopeless, everything else about us is sick. Where there is no hope, lethargy sets in and we begin to experience atrophy. The longer we are hopeless, the more negative we become. It is still amazing to me that we have the power to change all of the negatives we feel and may pass on to others unintentionally just by choosing to see things the way God does. We should not deny our circumstances, but neither should we give them permission to control our attitudes and behavior. God has given each of us power, and we can live above our circumstances, but only if we choose to have a hopeful, positive perspective.

If you decide to view things that are considered problems in a positive way, I can assure you that someone will promptly tell you that you aren't being realistic. But the good thing about faith is that it keeps you joyful and energized while you are trusting God to change the current reality. Someone may even say, "Don't be so childish," but that is exactly what God tells us we need to be if we intend to enjoy the life He provides. In Anne Frank's case, her amazingly good attitude didn't ever deliver her from her circumstances; in fact, she and her family were discovered in their hiding place, and they were taken to a prison camp where she eventually died of typhus, just as many of the other children did.

So you might say, "What good did her positive perspective do her?" I am certain that she was much happier than many of the people around her were. She kept a diary of her days as much as she could, and when it was discovered after the war, it was eventually translated into seventy languages and is now one of the most widely read accounts of the Holocaust. I know that her attitude has inspired millions of people and helped them make it through their difficulties. That alone is a good thing, and we can always find something good if we take the time to look.

The apostle Paul suffered greatly. He was beaten several times and imprisoned on a number of occasions for no crime other than believing in Jesus Christ and encouraging others to do the same. There are several verses of Scripture in 2 Corinthians 4 that I would like to quote and make some comments on.

> *We are hedged in (pressed) on every side [troubled and oppressed in every way], but not cramped or crushed; we suffer embarrassments and are perplexed and unable to find a way out, but not driven to despair.*
>
> *We are pursued (persecuted and hard driven), but not deserted [to stand alone]; we are struck down to the ground, but never struck out and destroyed.*

2 Corinthians 4:8–9

It doesn't sound like Paul's circumstances could have been much worse, and yet in the midst of them, we see a glimmer of hope and an attitude that refused to give up and cave in to a negative mind-set. Anyone who will refuse to give up no matter how challenging life may be is a far better and more powerful person than someone who is without challenges.

I often say that I have had two types of faith in my life, and I believe we need both of them. One is the type of faith that asks for and receives an immediate pleasurable answer. God delivers quickly and miraculously, and we get very excited. The second type of faith is one that doesn't receive the answer it had hoped for, but continues to believe anyway that God is good and that He is working in ways that cannot yet be seen. Although not as emotionally exciting, it is my personal opinion that the second type of faith is the greater faith. We don't get to choose which way God will work. At times He delivers us from something difficult, and at other times He gives us grace to endure it with a good attitude. What God does or does not allow us to go through is His decision and His alone, because He knows and understands things that we don't.

We live life forward, but we can only understand it backward. When we are going through something, it may make no sense at all. The pain we feel disables us from understanding, and yet later on, we can look back at the painful events and clearly understand that God's choice was better for us than what we would have chosen. There is also the possibility that we will never understand, but even then the heart of faith bows in worship, knowing that trust requires that we may always have some unanswered questions.

> *Therefore we do not become discouraged (utterly spiritless, exhausted, and wearied out through fear). Though our outer man is [progressively] decaying and wasting away, yet our inner self is being [progressively] renewed day after day.*
>
> *For our light, momentary affliction (this slight distress of the passing hour) is ever more and more abundantly preparing and producing and achieving for us an everlasting weight of glory [beyond all measure, excessively surpassing all comparisons and all calculations, a vast and transcendent glory and blessedness never to cease!].*
>
> 2 Corinthians 4:16–17

If I were to say what Paul was saying, it might sound like this:

> I am not going to let the fear of what may happen make me give up. I can see that my circumstances aren't great and they are taking a toll on my body, but something wonderful is taking place inside of me. In the private chambers of my soul, I feel strong, as if I am growing spiritually. I believe I am becoming a better person.
>
> What is happening now won't last forever. This too shall pass, and it will leave a deposit of something glorious—something that I could have never planned or even imagined.

If it will help you, why not copy this translation I have offered and put it someplace where you can read it easily anytime you need a perspective adjustment. It may help you refocus your life lens and see like Paul did.

To put the finishing touches on Paul's perspective, he says this:

> *Since we consider and look not to the things that are seen but to the things that are unseen; for the things that are visible are temporal (brief and fleeting), but the things that are invisible are deathless and everlasting.*
>
> 2 Corinthians 4:18

When what I see is discouraging me, I often go to these Scriptures and remember that there are things I cannot see with my natural eyes. They are far better things than what I am able to see. It is our choice—we can choose to believe God's promises and expect something good to happen, or not to believe—but I highly recommend believing. It has always proven to be the best way to live!

Think About It!

- You can be quick to see all the problems and magnify them, or you can make a choice to minimize the impact of difficulty by looking for the beauty, the good in life, and the good in people.
- Jesus is greater than any storm you will ever face.
- Your attitude can make a problem harder to deal with or easier—the choice is up to you.
- The best way to change your mood is to change your perspective.
- Trust requires that we may always have some unanswered questions.

CHAPTER 11

What Do You Think About That Person?

Be honest in your judgment and do not decide at a glance (superficially and by appearances); but judge fairly and righteously.

John 7:24

We spend much more time focusing on what people might be thinking about us than we do realizing what we are thinking about them. This is an arena of thought that is so important but often overlooked.

Have you ever met anyone you immediately disliked? We all have, but how could we honestly dislike someone that we barely know, or perhaps don't know at all? It is because we have let an attitude or a mind-set affect our feelings and opinions without even examining where the thought came from or why we have it. An insecure woman could meet a very beautiful woman and feel a dislike for her simply because she feels threatened by her good looks. It is important that we get to the root of these problems because God's Word teaches us not to judge at a glance, or superficially.

This will be easy for me to write on because it is a problem I have had in my life. I make very quick decisions, and that can be a problem when it comes to relationships. I spent many years not even examining why I didn't like some people; I just didn't and that was that. The sad thing is that they usually feel our dislike or rejection. If we don't reveal it in what we say, we do with voice tones, facial expressions, or body language. I will even go so far as to say that I believe people can feel the impact of our thoughts even though they don't know exactly what we are thinking.

I frequently tell the story of a woman who wrote to me telling me how she had a plant in her home that was not very attractive and each time she walked by it, she thought, *This is really an ugly plant*. It looked worse and worse as the days went by and it finally died. After hearing my teaching on the power of thoughts, she remembered the plant and thought perhaps she had influenced it in some way.

Some people say there is no scientific research to support such an idea, but many others who spend time in their gardens do talk to their plants. England's Prince Charles stated in 1986 that he went to his garden each day and talked to his plants. He obviously had plenty of people to talk to, so he surely wasn't doing it because he was lonely. He said if you talk to your plants they will respond and that it is important to talk to them. The theory that talking to plants makes them healthy dates back to 1848. Books have been written on the subject, and a music album was recorded for plants, based on the thought that the music would help them grow and be healthy.[1]

As the woman who sent me the letter considered how her negative thoughts about the plant influenced her, she realized that she regularly thought negative thoughts about her mother-in-law, who rarely called her—and she had no kind words for her even when she did. She decided to do an experiment, so she purposely began thinking kind thoughts about her mother-in-law. Only a few days went by and she received a phone call from her, during which she actually was more friendly than usual and began doling out compliments over the course of time. The end of the story is that they became good friends!

Many years ago, I was with one of my daughters, who was a teenager at the time. Her hair looked quite strange that day (in my opinion), and she had some acne on her face that she had tried too hard to hide with makeup. The excessive makeup only called attention to the problem she was trying to hide. As we spent the day together, I must admit that each time I looked at her I thought, *You sure don't look good today—your hair is a mess and you have way too much makeup on.* As the day went by, I noticed that she appeared to be getting depressed. I ask her what was wrong and she said, "I just feel really ugly today!" It took God only about one millisecond to tell me it was my fault. Ouch! But He was right, as He always is, and it was a lesson on the power of thoughts that I will never forget.

I am not saying that people can read our minds, but I do think that somehow our thoughts, good or bad, have an impact on those around us. They certainly show on our face, in our body language, and in our behavior toward people. Be more careful of the thoughts you think about people when you are with them and when you are not. Why? Because thoughts prepare us for action. Where the mind goes, the man follows! It is impossible for me to think evil thoughts about someone when I am not with them and then be kind and friendly when I see them. I might fake it, but any astute person would realize something wasn't right even if they didn't know what it was.

> Thoughts prepare us for action.

Give People a Chance

If we take time to get to know people a little more intimately, we may like them more. There are lots of reasons why we decide too quickly that we don't like someone, but none of them are valid. Perhaps they have a personality type that we don't enjoy, or they may have a personality that reminds us of someone who has hurt us in the past. We may make decisions about them based on the way they look, their hairstyle, or the automobile they drive, or how they are dressed. It took me a few years to realize that I rejected people who reminded me of my father. He was gruff, negative, and generally unfriendly, so I preferred people who had none of those traits, even though I was that way myself. If Dave had not looked beyond my exterior, we would have never even had a first date.

The first time Dave saw me, I was washing my mother's car in front of our house, and he was picking up a neighbor to give him a ride somewhere. He decided to flirt with me and said, "Hey, when you are finished washing that car, would you like to wash mine?" I replied very firmly, and with a matter-of-fact tone of voice, "If you want your car washed, wash it yourself!" However, my rough exterior did not dissuade Dave. He has often shared that it intrigued him, and he decided on the spot that I was the girl for him. All I can say is that he definitely had mastered the ability to believe the best of people. Soon after that encounter, he asked me for a date, and after five dates, he asked me to marry him (he was a fast worker)! I often say that God led him to marry me before he had time to discover how many problems I had that he would have to patiently help me work through over the next few years. We have been married since 1967, but if he had judged superficially, or at a glance, we would have missed a wonderful opportunity to serve God together.

I wonder how many women want to get married, but they reject man after man because those men don't fit into the preconceived idea women carry of "Mr. Right." I also wonder how many men want to marry, but reject every woman they are not immediately attracted to. There is a lot more to everyone than meets the eye. Everyone has a story, and if we would take time to know people better, we would see them differently than we might otherwise.

Let's say that Sally had been praying for quite some time that God would lead her to the man she would marry. She was in her late thirties, was lonely, and very much wanted a husband. A friend arranged a date for her with John, but she took one look at him and flatly decided he was *not* the man for her. He was a blue-collar worker, didn't have a college degree, and besides that, he was no taller than she was and about ten pounds overweight. He wasn't what she had in mind!

A few weeks later she was introduced to Jack. He was tall and handsome, had graduated from an Ivy League college, and was quickly climbing the ladder of success as an investment broker. Within a few months they were married, but within a year they were divorced. Sally didn't know that Jack had a violent temper, was manipulative and controlling, and had a gambling problem. She had been so impressed by his superficial qualities that even though she had noticed some of the flaws, she made excuses for all of them and said "I do" for all the wrong reasons.

Sally was brokenhearted, felt like a failure, was more lonely than ever, and extremely discouraged. On a Saturday morning, she was sitting alone at a coffee shop, watching the rain drizzle down, when she looked up and saw John, the man she had quickly rejected because she didn't like his superficial qualities.

John stopped to say hello, and because he was a sensitive, caring man, he quickly noticed that Sally was hurting emotionally. John began to call her to check up on her. He sent her flowers for no reason other than to cheer her up. He offered her a listening ear, kindness, and understanding. Before long, Sally realized that he was a man of integrity and good character. He used wisdom with money, and although he was not yet forty years old, he owned a new car and a very nice small home, and was debt free. Sally soon fell deeply in love with John, and none of the things that had initially bothered her concerned her at all now. She could have saved herself a divorce, a lot of mental and emotional agony, and a year of misery if she had had the wisdom to get to know people better before accepting or rejecting them.

Is there anyone you have decided you just don't like and have shut out of your life without ever really taking time to know them? I am sure the answer is yes for most of us. A lot of people complain that they don't have any friends or that they are lonely, but perhaps they are too quick to decide who they will let into their lives and who they won't.

That person at work whom you avoid all the time, because you have already decided you don't like them, could be hurting and in need of your friendship or a listening ear. They could even be the friend you have been asking God to give you, but you will never know if you don't give them a chance.

I can think of numerous people I have been initially unimpressed with, and now that I am asking myself why, I must admit that I don't have any good reasons. One is a man I see at a coffee shop fairly regularly. He is an elderly man with very long white hair, and he seems a bit unique. (Of course, I am assuming in my pride that I am the standard for normal. *Ouch!*) One day I thought, *What if this man is an angel?* After all, the Bible does say that sometimes we are entertaining angels unaware (see Hebrews 13:2). That may be too much of a stretch for some of you, but I am willing to go there in my thinking. Now that I think about it, his long white hair is a bit angelic!

Jesus was rejected by lots of people because He was a unique individual. It is humorous to think that the most religious people of the day, the Pharisees, rejected the Son of God! John the Baptist was certainly unique—he roamed around the desert dressed like a wild man, eating wild locust and honey, and preaching things that people were not accustomed to hearing. Truthfully, many of God's choice servants are people you and I would have never chosen for the job God assigns them. I think you are getting the point. Lots of amazing people don't fit into our "thought mold" of what they should be. I want people to give me a chance and take time to get to know the real me, so I have decided that I am going to try harder to do the same thing for them.

Jesus didn't choose to help or befriend people based on how others perceived them. Everyone was shocked when Jesus went to Zacchaeus' house, because Zacchaeus was a chief tax collector, and tax collectors were not only hated but were also known for their dishonesty. Why would Jesus do that? Was He purposely trying to ruin His reputation? Truthfully, He did not care what people thought of Him, but I am sure He was very careful what He thought about other people. He gave Zacchaeus a chance, and because He did, Zacchaeus solemnly declared that he would give half of his goods to restore to people what he had dishonestly taken (see Luke 19:1–8). Lots of people would blossom into something better than what they currently are if we would just give them a chance.

Jesus touched lepers, and that was something nobody else did (see Matthew 8). He talked to a needy woman at the well, and Jewish men did not talk to Samaritan women (see John 4). He traveled with a woman who had previously had seven demons and made her living as a prostitute (see Luke 8). He chose disciples we would have surely rejected as unfit for the job, and He ate with "publicans and sinners" (see Matthew 9:11 KJV). Jesus broke all the rules of the day and gave us a new one: Love one another, just as He loves you (see John 13:34).

> *Jesus broke all the rules of the day and gave us a new one: Love one another, just as He loves you.*

First Impressions

In a *Christianity Today* article, Stephen Brown quoted F. B. Meyer when he wrote that there are two things we do not know about other people: First, we do not know how hard he or she tried not to sin. And second, we do not know the power of the forces that assailed him or her.[2] One thing I would add is that we also do not know what we would have done in the same circumstances.

What we think about others greatly impacts how we relate to them. Our thoughts about a person affect how we treat them, and how we allow that person to treat us. A person may want to do something kind for us, but if we have already decided that we don't trust them, we may shut a door of opportunity that God is trying to open.

I read that, in 1884, parents who were grieving the loss of their son decided to establish a memorial to him. They went to Harvard University and met with the president, Charles Eliot. Eliot is purported to have been surprised when the simple, unpretentious people asked about funding a building in their son's name. He discouraged them from the idea, saying that it would be way too expensive. He assumed they didn't have the money and suggested they do something simple and less costly. The couple declined and left without making a donation.

Only a year later, Eliot was informed that the same couple he had dismissed unceremoniously had established a $26 million memorial named Leland Stanford Junior University, known to you and me today as Stanford.[3]

Eliot missed a great blessing due to making improper assumptions based on first impressions. His unkind thoughts and attitude about the couple cost him more than he could have imagined at the time.

It is very important to see people the way God sees them. First Samuel 16:7 says: "For the Lord sees not as man sees; for man looks on the outward appearance, but the Lord looks on the heart." If we are willing, we can learn to think about people the way God thinks about them. We'll recognize each person as a valuable possibility instead of a potential problem.

To see people the way God sees them, and to think about them the way that God thinks about them, comes with spiritual maturity—it is a by-product of walking in the Spirit rather than walking in the flesh. It is often a sacrifice, because we may not want to take the time to know them more deeply. I realize that we cannot be best friends with everyone we meet, but we can at least stop being rude to people by evaluating them at a glance. There will always be people we can relate to better than others, but that should not be an excuse for having an exclusive attitude. We may all benefit by widening our circle of inclusion.

Our fleshly mind makes judgments about people—right or wrong—based upon first impressions. Within minutes, we form thoughts about a person that can sabotage a relationship before it ever begins.

Mother Teresa said, "If you judge people, you have no time

to love them."[4] A Roman poet, Phaedrus, said, "Things are not always what they seem; the first appearance deceives many."[5] I admit that first impressions are important and we should all try to make a good one, but everyone deserves a second chance.

The problem of judging by first impressions without having all the facts can be a problem even with people who love God and are very serious about serving Him. John Wesley is considered to be a great man of God, and yet even he made this mistake.

One day Wesley scolded a man who gave only a small gift to a worthy charity. After being rebuked, the man explained to Wesley that he wasn't giving as little as he could; he was giving as much as he could. In fact, the man had been living on only parsnips and water for several weeks.

The poor man went on to tell Wesley that before his conversion, he had run up several bills. Now he was skimping on necessities and refusing any personal luxuries so that he could pay off his creditors one at a time. The man said, "Christ has made me an honest man, and so with all these debts to pay, I can give only a few offerings above my tithe." He went on to explain to Wesley that he felt compelled to settle his debts in order to show his worldly creditors how the grace of God can change a man's heart.

John Wesley was convicted and apologized to the man immediately.[6]

Jesus saw things differently. He noticed a widow putting into the offering two "mites," as they were called in those days (see Luke 21:1–4). There are various opinions about exactly how much that would amount to in today's economy, but we know it was a very small amount. Jesus saw more than the amount of money she was giving; He saw that she was giving all she had. Let's make a commitment to look deeper than the surface appearances of people and situations. Let's pray before going out into the world each day that God would help us not to form our thoughts and opinions of people too quickly, lest we shut them out of our lives and miss the opportunity to know the amazing people God has placed in our path.

Think About It!

- The way we think about people affects how we treat them.
- Every person has a story. If you get to know them, you might begin to think of them in a different light.
- Jesus loved people, and He instructs us to do the same.
- With God's help, our first response to people can be to love them instead of to judge them.

CHAPTER 12

Anybody Can Change

With men [it is] impossible, but not with God; for all things are possible with God.

Mark 10:27

The best way to kill a relationship is to look at the other person and think, *You will never change.* Thankfully, God always believes we can change, and therefore, He continues to work with us. We would be more patient and long-suffering with the flaws of people if we purposely thought, *God is patient with me and I will be patient with you.* We can always choose to pray for people instead of giving up on them.

The first few years of my marriage to Dave, my behavior was at its worst. I had never been in a healthy relationship and honestly had no idea how to behave in one. My thoughts about marriage, and what to expect from a relationship, were all warped and unrealistic. Here are some examples of some of the wrong thinking I had:

- *Dave needs to make me feel good about myself.*
- *Dave needs to do more things to make me happy.*
- *Someone needs to pay me back for the abuse in my childhood.*
- *I don't trust men.*
- *Dave doesn't talk enough.*

- *Dave doesn't give me enough compliments.*
- *Dave doesn't bring me gifts.*
- *Dave is too involved in sports.*

I am sure you can see the problem. All my thoughts were about what I needed and how Dave needed to focus on me and do everything I wanted him to do. I must say that I was totally self-absorbed, but I was also totally unaware that there was any other way to live. My experience to that point in life was that nobody really cared about me, or was going to take care of me, so it was my job to look out for myself. If I didn't do it, nobody would. I expected things from Dave that God would not allow him to give me, because I was looking to the wrong person. God wants to be our source and, although He does use other people to encourage and help us, He wants us to lean and rely on Him rather than them.

It is surprising that Dave was able to stay with me during those years. I am sure he felt defeated at times, because no matter what he did, I wasn't happy. I could not have ever been happy, no matter what my circumstances were, because everything going on inside of me was wrong. My thoughts and attitudes were all wrong, and that controlled my moods and behaviors. I thought about me. I thought about what was wrong with me. What was wrong with other people. What was wrong with life. I thought about what people were not doing for me. How unfairly I had been treated most of my life. I was almost paranoid about what people thought of me.

You don't have to be a genius to see what my problem was. When I have asked Dave what enabled him to stick with me, he says, "I knew that God could change you!" Wow! He had to be a man of faith. His belief that God could change me was a key factor in my healing. I didn't know how to trust God yet, so He used Dave to do it for me. His faith opened a door for God to work in my life. Those years were not easy on Dave, and he has said that he often wept about our situation, but no matter how difficult things were, *he always believed that God could change me.*

It is obvious that there are people who don't change, but they could change if they would open their hearts and let God in. Nobody is beyond change! It may take a long time for them to do so, but it can happen. My father was in his eighties when he finally apologized to me for his abusive behavior and asked for forgiveness from me and from God. He received Christ, and I saw a genuine change in him. I am glad I didn't give up, but that doesn't mean that I wasn't tempted to, or that there were not times when I did for a season. But the Holy Spirit would always stir me up again by reminding me that although no person could change my father, nothing was impossible with God.

> *Nobody is beyond change! It may take a long time for them to do so, but it can happen.*

I wasn't in a relationship with my father during some of those years, because it would not have been wise or safe for me or my children. But faith transcends distance, and we can trust God to do what is impossible with men no matter what our geographical location is. I suggest that you pray for people who need to let God into their lives and then "say what you pray." If you are praying for someone, then don't go to lunch with a friend and talk about how you doubt that they will ever change. It is also destructive to look at the person you are praying for and perhaps in a time of anger shout at them, "You will never change."

Even if you see no change at all yet, you can continue believing that God is working and guide your conversations with others in that direction. Fill your mind with thoughts like *I believe God is working and all things are possible with Him*. You will feel better, and your attitude toward the person in question will be much better.

Do We Give Up Too Easily?

According to God's Word, "love endures long" (see 1 Corinthians 13:4). I was not able to love my father as a real father, or have kind and pleasurable feelings toward him, but I could still love him with the love of Christ. God loves us whether or not we ever love Him back, and that is a totally different kind of love than what we normally think love is. Romantic love, parental love, and the love we have for friends are all based, at least in part, on what others do for us, and how they treat us. God's love is based on who He is and His decision to love us unconditionally.

I think it is important that we understand the difference in these various types of love. In our English language, we use the word *love* for lots of things. We *love* vacations, movies, ice cream, and our families, but each requires a different commitment. God's love is referred to in the Greek language as *agape*, and we can have that when all the other types of love have vanished.

God placed His love in Dave's heart when he was a young boy, and it was with that love that Dave loved me. God gives us His love, and it enables us to love others. It enables us to endure some difficulties and be the type of people who don't give up.

I think to endure means to outlast the problem. Dave endured. He outlasted my problems! I endured and outlasted my father's problems. If you have given up on someone, you can make a course correction right now and start believing that *God can change anybody*.

I have frequently had to go to this Scripture for comfort and courage to press on when I have become weary of dealing with a person who seems to never improve. This is one of the Scriptures that has encouraged me often:

> *Bear (endure, carry) one another's burdens and troublesome moral faults, and in this way fulfill and observe perfectly the law of Christ (the Messiah) and complete what is lacking [in your obedience to it].*
>
> Galatians 6:2

I have learned that I am not responsible for changing people; I am responsible only to fulfill the law of Christ, which is love! I think we focus too much on the results we are or are not getting from our sacrifices, instead of just being fulfilled in knowing that we are doing what God is asking of us and the results are up to Him. We should do what is right because it is right and not only to get results!

Avoid thinking that leads to weakness and giving up. Don't think:

- *This is too hard.*
- *I can't do this anymore.*
- *I will never change.*
- *It is too late for this to ever change.*

Believe that you can do anything God asks you to do through Christ (see Philippians 4:13).

We have all heard amazing stories of how people have been changed by God. Many of them involve God using someone who was willing to believe and not give up on them. Let God use you. Start believing that anybody can change.

Our job is not to try to change people, but to believe that God can change them. Are you trying to do God's job and in the process not doing your own? Dave shared that he knew God could change me, but he also knew that he himself couldn't, so he didn't try to. I can honestly say that I never felt a subtle threat from Dave that if I didn't change he would leave. I felt only love from him. Sadly, most of the time I couldn't receive it, but that didn't stop him from being who he was. He kept offering love, and he remained joyful. God keeps giving even if we have not yet learned how to receive, and we can learn to do the same thing in our relationships with other people.

A man we will call Bob, who was always a happy fellow, was waiting one cold winter morning for a bus. Another man was selling newspapers on the corner where he waited, and as usual, Bob offered a friendly greeting. The newspaperman scowled and said something rude to him, but Bob kept right on being friendly and happy. Another man who was also waiting for the bus asked Bob, "How can you just keep being friendly and nice to that man after the way he talked to you?" Bob responded, "Why should I let his unhappiness steal mine? I will pray for him and remain as I am."

Too often we let other people's problems and behavior change us, and that is one of the worst things we can do. It doesn't help us and it doesn't help them either.

Dave didn't let me make him unhappy, and that was eventually good for me. Through his example, I finally saw that a joy is available to us that is not dependent on other people or on our circumstances. I wanted that joy! But I would not have even known it existed if Dave had given up on me. He simply stayed and remained joyful. How many great opportunities do we miss in life simply because we give up too easily? I can assure you that if Dave had driven home from work at night thinking, *She is never going to change, and I can't take this much longer,* he would have missed many of the amazing opportunities God has given us over the years to use our testimony to encourage other people. We never get a testimony without going through a test!

> *We never get a testimony without going through a test!*

Stop Frustrating Yourself

I spent a lot of years frustrated most of the time, and thankfully, I now know how to avoid it. Frustration is always caused from what the Bible calls "works of the flesh," which is our human energy trying to do what only God can do. Stop trying to change things you cannot change, and frustration disappears. We have two options in life and they are to either struggle or trust God. Since we cannot change people, we can change our attitude toward them. Dave could have felt sorry for himself, but I think he realized how miserable I was and felt more sorry for me. He was able to see beyond how I made him feel to how unhappy I was. He felt true compassion for me, and it empowered him to not give up.

If Dave had been continually thinking bad thoughts about me, I would have felt the impact of them. I would have felt his rejection and negativity. However, as it was, I never felt any of that. I desperately needed to see Jesus, and Dave was showing me what He was like. Perhaps I was finally able to believe that I could change because I could sense that Dave believed I could.

Dave did confront me if I got what he called "too sassy" with him, but he definitely picked his battles, and he didn't confront me about every little thing I did wrong.

You can find almost unbelievable relief by facing the fact that you cannot change another person. Sometimes what we want from people is unrealistic, and we have to learn to let them be who they

> Controlling ourselves should be our goal, not controlling someone else.

are, but if they truly do need to change, God is the only One who can do it. Controlling ourselves should be our goal, not controlling someone else.

We Can't Change Ourselves by Ourselves

Even when an individual comes to the point that they want to change, they cannot do it alone. Only God can work from the inside out, and that is what we need. For any change in behavior to last, it must come from the heart. I can muster enough discipline to change some of my behavior, but only God can change my heart.

As I said, anyone can change, but God has to be invited to do the changing. Our job is to want to change, and God's job is to do the work while we believe and cooperate with His instructions.

The Bible says that when God gives your enemies over to you, then you must utterly destroy them (see Deuteronomy 7:1–2). I was struck by the realization that I could not destroy my enemies of anger, selfishness, bitterness, jealousy, and many others until God gave them to me. God deals with things in our life one at a time—if you get ahead of God, you will get very frustrated and confused. You will have no success; you will struggle and feel defeated. You will be discouraged and want to give up.

The Israelites could not leave the bondage they were in while imprisoned in Egypt until God's perfect time came. Joshua could not take Jericho until the exact right day. Jesus wasn't raised from the dead until the third day. Why the third day? Why not the first or second day? The simple, but often difficult, answer to receive is that it was just not the right time yet. We can believe that God is working, even when we don't see any evidence that He is. That is what faith is.

We may want someone to change before God is ready for that particular thing. There are many things that God knows of which we have no understanding at all. I have had to accept that my little corner of the world is not the only corner that exists. God works all things together for good, not just our things. I may be frustrated because God is not doing something that I think needs to be done, but He is working on someone or something else that has to be in place before He does the thing I am asking Him to do. God has a perfect way, a perfect plan, and a perfect time, and He will not be rushed. All things work together for good in due time.

Think of buying a five-thousand-piece puzzle. You buy it because you like the picture on the box, but when you dump out all the pieces on the table, you feel overwhelmed. All the things going on in our lives are a bit like that. We like the picture God presents in His Word of what we may become, but will we be patient enough to see the picture put together?

Patience

Even after I did start wanting to change and began working with God toward my restoration, Dave still had to be patient because I was a work in progress, just as we all are. When you're in relationship with someone who needs to change, or if you are the one who needs to change, be patient! Be happy for and celebrate the changes you do see no matter how small, and it will give you encouragement to press on and not give up. We are all still changing, including Dave and me.

Just three days ago, I said something to Dave in front of some of our friends that I should not have said. I firmly told him that he was wrong about something he said. I knew he didn't like it, but he didn't say anything to me. I knew immediately that I was wrong and couldn't wait to get in a place where I could apologize to him. Yesterday, I asked Dave to do something fairly minor for me, but it would have meant that he had to adjust his plans a little, and he said a firm "No!" I left it in God's hands and went on about my business, and soon he came and apologized.

In both of these instances, God was given the opportunity to convict us of wrong behavior, and the situations were rectified quickly. But we often try to convince someone of bad behavior—we start an argument and nothing is ever solved. If we were more patient and willing to be quiet and wait on God, a lot of changes would take place more quickly. It is amazing how powerfully God can work when we are silent! The Holy Spirit is the One who convicts of sin and convinces us of righteousness (see John 16:8).

Patience and prayer working together accomplish great things, and we keep our peace while those things are getting done. God can do in a moment what we cannot accomplish in a lifetime!

Changes I Have Seen

I regret that there are people I have given up on over the years because I didn't think they would ever change. Now I know that with God, all things are possible. I have seen some amazing changes in myself and other family members and friends. All of my children have turned out better than I imagined they would have when they were teenagers at home and driving me crazy. I won't go into all the details, but each of them had their own unique set of "drive mom crazy" traits, which I was sure would prevent them from ever being productive adults.

Now two of our sons run the day-to-day activities of Joyce Meyer Ministries as well as all the media, the missions, and the management operations. One of our daughters is homeschooling her children, as well as being busy in ministry as often as possible. Our other daughter assists me part-time, helping keep my life organized. By the way, she was the one who was so disorganized growing up that I thought she wouldn't even be able to find herself once she left home.

As for the changes in me . . . *wow*! I am not even the same person I once was. I joke that Dave has been married to at least twenty versions of me over the forty-eight years we have been together. I sincerely want to encourage you one last time to believe that anyone can change. As I said earlier, you may not be able to be in a relationship with them the whole time they are deciding if they want to change or not, but you can still be very influential in their progress by praying and believing that change is possible with God. When you see or think of people you know who are difficult to deal with, don't think of or talk about them as if they will never change! Try saying, "God, I believe _____ can change, and I ask You to keep working with them until they do."

Think About It!

- Nobody is beyond change. It may take a long time, but it can happen.
- We can love others because God loves us. He sets the perfect example of how to love.
- To endure means to outlast the problem. If you're waiting for change to occur, don't give up.
- We can't change the people in our lives—only God can bring about real and lasting change.
- Supernatural change always comes from the inside out.

CHAPTER 13

Why Aren't You Like Me?

Having gifts (faculties, talents, qualities) that differ according to the grace given us, let us use them.

Romans 12:6

Did you ever look at someone and think, *What is wrong with you?* I have, and I am sure you have too. Why would we think that? It is usually because the person we are thinking about is simply not like we are.

When it comes to having good relationships, it is vital that we learn to accept the differences in all people. God creates us all differently on purpose. Those who are different from you are not just people who got in all the wrong lines when God was passing out personality traits. I have a friend who is so nice that I am surprised her name is not "Sugar." I am working on it, but I doubt I will ever be as naturally nice as she is. I have thought, *Where was I when God handed out the "nice genes"?* I was right where I was supposed to be, getting what God wanted me to have, and so were you and everyone else. Let's remember that God created each of us in our mother's womb carefully and intricately (see Psalm 139:13–16). We are not mistakes just because we are not like someone else.

Two of my granddaughters from the same set of parents are

> God creates us all differently on purpose.

thirteen and fifteen years old. They don't look alike, and they don't act alike. One of them is a lot like me in looks and personality, and the other one is the exact opposite. One is a bottom-line, no-nonsense, and no-frills type of person. If you ask her a question, you had better be ready for her honest opinion, because she won't try to soften the blow if what you are about to hear isn't encouraging. The other girl is so sweet she drips with sweetness, and no matter what she says to you, she somehow makes it sound good.

If I were to ask Emily, the thirteen-year-old, if she liked my outfit and she didn't, she would say, "No!" If I ask Abigail, the fifteen-year-old, if she didn't like it, she might say something like, "Grandma, almost everything looks really good on you, and that one is all right, but you have things that make you look stunning!"

My daughter, Laura, asked Emily the other day what she was studying in history and her answer was, "People." "Oh," said Laura, and after a long pause she decided she would try again to stir up some conversation and said, "What time period are the people from?" and Emily answered, "Early." If she had asked Abigail that same question, they would have had a thirty- to forty-five-minute discussion that included every tiny detail. Laura called me and we had a good laugh. It was a fresh reminder of just how different we all are and how important it is to accept that fact.

Thinking everyone should be like us is one of our biggest problems in relationships, and it causes a lot of wrong thinking and wrong attitudes that are damaging to healthy and satisfying marriages, friendships, and work relationships.

It still amazes me how much trouble I had getting along with people until I learned the important lesson that I am not the perfect standard for how people should be. You are probably thinking, *Joyce, you sure had a lot of problems.* Yes, I did, and I am glad I have been able to be honest with myself about them, because only the truth sets us free. I have enjoyed a lot of victory and many wonderful breakthroughs and positive changes, and I know that anyone who wants to can also have the same thing.

Dave and I were shopping one time when he found a blouse he liked and was astonished when I didn't like it. "What is wrong with it? How could you not like this? It would look great on you," he said. There would have been a time in my life when I would have either felt that perhaps something was wrong with me because I didn't like it, or I would have pretended I liked it just to make him happy, or I would have gotten angry because I felt he was trying to make me like it. None of those are good choices! But now I simply said (sweetly, of course), "I just don't like it," and I moved on to the next store. It is very freeing when we know who we are in Christ and we have the confidence to be the person He made us to be.

I don't feel the need to apologize for how I see things and what I like or don't like. Of course, in order to have that freedom, I need to give freedom to others, and I have learned to do so. I am still growing, of course, but at least I understand the importance of the principle and how it affects relationships.

The Boredom of Sameness

If everyone in life were the same, you would be bored. The truth is that God has created us all differently on purpose, and although I don't always understand why He created some people the way He did, I do know I am called by Him to love and accept them and not to think something is wrong with them because they don't fit into my idea of "normal." God loves variety and we should learn to love it also.

Just think how boring life would be if everyone and everything looked and behaved exactly alike. What if all people looked alike and had the same temperament? What if every tree and flower were the same, and every bird, dog, cat, et cetera? Boring! We can learn to appreciate the variety of people God has placed in the world, and we can learn how to think about the differences in people in a way that honors God and improves our relationships.

How many people do we shut out of our lives, exclude, and criticize, making them feel inferior just because they are not like us? Probably more than we would care to count. We all connect with some people more than others, but even if we don't want to be a person's best friend, we can appreciate their uniqueness as God's creation and make every effort to never make them feel insignificant.

Significance

One of the top needs that all people have is to feel significant. We want to feel that we matter, that we have value and purpose. Acceptance from others helps to make us feel that way. We can accept or reject someone without saying a word. I have been thinking about my facial expressions when someone or something they do seems strange to me. I open my eyes real wide, as if to say, *You think what?* I scrunch up my mouth, which then pushes my nose into a different position, and that says without words, *What is your problem?* Sometimes I shake my head in disbelief, indicating that I absolutely cannot believe the person did a thing, thinks a thing, or is doing a thing that I would not do. All of this is accomplished without words. If I add sighs, moans, groans, gasps, and descriptive body language, I have found several other ways to let people know I think something is wrong with them, and I still haven't said a word.

If I do start talking to the person or about the person concerning their "ways," I can do some major damage. The frightening thing is that I can do and have done all of that, and not even given it a second thought. Wow! I am really sorry I've behaved this way, and I am more committed than ever to making people feel valuable.

Making people feel significant begins with how we think about them. We need to take time to consider how we think about the people in our lives. Is there anyone we approve of 100 percent? Probably not, but the percentage would go way up if we just realize they don't need to be like us. They don't have to think what we think, like what we like, share our opinions, or make the same choices we would in situations. God loves and accepts all of us, and He desires that we do the same thing with one another.

> Making people feel significant begins with how we think about them.

When someone has a totally different opinion from ours, instead of giving them a look like they are an alien from another planet, why not look at them and think, *I respect your right to your opinion, and I realize that the way I see things may not be right all the time.* If we think that way, we will talk that way and behave that way. When we tell someone about an idea we have and they offer one that is very different from ours, why not look at them and think with a smile, *I am open to other ideas, and I will consider yours.* This would be preferable to opening your mouth without any thought and blurting out, "Do you always have to disagree with me? That is the stupidest idea I have ever heard. Surely you don't really think that would work?!"

Try making a list of the people that you deal with in life the most, and then go over the list often and do some "on-purpose thinking." Think things like this on purpose: *[Person's name] is valuable, they are gifted, and I need the variety they offer to my life. I appreciate their uniqueness, and I want to help them be all they can be.*

Taking this positive viewpoint about people doesn't mean that they have nothing in their personalities that needs to be changed or polished, but it does mean that we agree not to see ourselves as being more important and valuable than others. It also means that we agree that God is wise, and since He seems to love variety, then we need to embrace it also.

What Did God Have in Mind?

If you ask questions, you will find that most married people are married to someone who is vastly different from them in temperament. If people have multiple children, those children are all different from one another. We work with people that are all different, go to school with them, live in neighborhoods with them. What did God have in mind? He wants us to need and depend on each other. He gives each of us a part of the whole, but nobody gets it all. God gives each of us abilities and talents that differ from other people's. Dave and I are soooooo different, but we stopped fighting about it long, long ago. Be wise enough to accept what you cannot change and realize that God has a plan. Submit to it and you will begin to benefit from it. God has given me *exactly* what I need in giving me Dave, but for way too many years, I only found fault with the things about him I didn't like, instead of finding the value in what I did like.

Dave and I talk often about how great our relationship is now, and how it is good because we give each other the freedom to be our own unique selves. Don't waste all the time we did and spin your wheels trying to make the people in your life be something they don't know how to be. Learn from my mistakes and enjoy life sooner than I did.

You may be thinking of the things you don't like about someone, and even my suggestion of acceptance makes you fume. If so, I totally understand. I am not suggesting that we accept sinful behavior and applaud it, but I am urging you to accept other things that probably are not going to change. For instance, if your spouse or friend is quiet and you're a talker, just be glad you have someone quiet enough to listen to you instead of telling them that they need to talk more. If you are aggressive and in a relationship with someone who is more laid-back and relaxed, be glad you have someone who will probably peacefully go along with most of what you want to do. I recall saying to Dave one time, "You need to be more aggressive." He said, "You better be glad that I am the way I am or you would not be doing the things you are doing!" I saw the light! He was right—God had given me the right guy for the unique situation that we have.

I think sometimes we have difficulty in relationships because we have a worldview of how everyone should be. I may not be a normal wife or mother according to the accepted world standard, but I am a good one, and I believe I am one who is following God's plan. Dave may not be like, or do all the things other husbands do, but he is awesome, happy, peaceful, amazing, and just right for me. Stop trying to put yourself or someone else into a box that they will never fit into and start celebrating your uniqueness.

Remember that the mind is connected to everything else. If you want better relationships, examine how you think about the people in your life. Ask God to help you see them the way that He does and to think about them the way that He does, and I can promise you that you will be happier and your relationships will improve.

What Do You Think of Me?

At the beginning of this section I said that we should spend more time thinking about what we think of other people than we do about what they think of us. I just saw someone from the neighborhood who asked me if I was going to participate in a cleanup day the area had organized. I responded that I would not be, but later I found myself wondering what she thought of me because I wasn't helping. I knew that my reason for not helping was a valid one, but I was concerned about what she thought. I know the agony of being a people pleaser, so I started thinking about the instruction in God's Word to focus on pleasing God, not on pleasing people (see Galatians 1:10; Ephesians 6:6). This helped me to immediately refocus and get back on the right track mentally.

Do you ever get caught in the trap of thinking too much about what people are thinking and saying about you? I think most of us do at times. We want people to like us, to think well of us, and to accept us, and that is quite normal; however, if we are not careful, we can let concern for what people think of us begin to control us and cause us to lose sight of God's plan for us.

What I think about other people is more important than what they are thinking about me! I am not responsible for their thoughts, but I am responsible before God for mine. So I decided to think some *on-purpose thoughts* about the neighbor that were good and beneficial. For example: *She seems like a very nice woman! She appears to be in her sixties but is in good physical shape! I like her hairstyle! She is friendly!* I knew from experience that if I purposed to think good things about her instead of worrying about what she was thinking about me, I would respond to her better the next time I saw her. If I continued to be worried about her thoughts about me, the next time I saw her I would have responded insecurely, halfway expecting her to say something critical about me not being able to participate in the cleanup day. But by meditating on good things about her, I knew I would enjoy seeing her again and would have a few compliments ready for her, because they would already have been in my thoughts.

How to Think About People

How we think about people when we are not with them determines how we will treat them when we are. I really want to please God concerning how I make people feel, and I am sure you feel the same way. I have spent many years letting the Holy Spirit teach me how to treat people, and one thing I am still learning is the vital role my thoughts play in the outcome of every relationship. It is exciting to me to realize that I can prepare myself for action by choosing my thoughts carefully. If I don't want to mistreat people and leave them feeling bad after being in my presence, then I will need to think good things about them before our time together as well as during it.

> How we think about people when we are not with them determines how we will treat them when we are.

Remember that people don't always remember what we say, but they do remember how we made them feel. Plan to make them feel good. Another female leader and I were discussing how we want to grow in appreciating other people's ideas more. We are both strong-willed and decisive, and when we are in meetings and people have ideas that seem unreasonable to us, we both find it difficult to keep what we are thinking off our faces. Even if we stay quiet, the face can tell all. I shared with her that I believed we could prepare ourselves to have good facial reactions to opinions that differ from ours by purposely planning how we would respond ahead of time. We should pray that God helps us think of people the way we would want them to think of us.

Before going into a creative meeting where we know different opinions are going to be abundantly and openly shared, we can think things like *There will be lots of different opinions offered today and they are all heartfelt and worth considering.* Or, *Everyone in the room is valuable, and I am going to treat them as if they are.* Or, *When anyone shares an idea that I don't like, I am going to remember that they have a right to their opinion, even if I don't happen to agree with it.*

There are countless ways that we can benefit from aggressive, positive, on-purpose thinking about people. Before meeting with anyone, even a friend for coffee, think of the things you enjoy and appreciate about them. Most of us don't have to try to think of the things we don't like—they come to our minds uninvited—but we can give them no entrance by already having our minds filled with good things. For example, *I am having lunch with a friend in a month. I am thrilled that I have a month to think good things about her, and I can't wait to see the positive effect it has on our time together.*

Prayer Thoughts

Prayer is what makes every venture successful, and we can combine our prayers and thoughts and accomplish two goals at one time. While thinking good things about any event or person, we can turn those thoughts into prayers offered simply to our Heavenly Father. Try it! "Father, I know that You love _____, and I appreciate all the strengths you have given them. They are fun to be with, encouraging, and helpful. Thank You for putting them in my life."

Relationships are a major part of our lives, and I pray that we will always remember how much our thoughts affect them. Be aggressively positive in how you think about all people. All people (including us) do have faults and weaknesses, but thankfully, with God's help, we can focus on their strengths.

Think About It!

- It is vital that we learn to accept the differences in all people.
- God created each person to be unique. Life would be boring if everyone and everything looked and acted the same.
- Making people feel significant begins in how we think about them.
- The mind is connected to everything else. If you want better relationships, examine how you think about the people in your life.
- People don't always remember what you say, but they do remember how you made them feel.

SECTION 3

How Your Thoughts Affect Your Physical and Emotional Health

CHAPTER 14

Your Thoughts and Stress

Lean on, trust in, and be confident in the Lord with all your heart and mind and do not rely on your own insight or understanding.

Proverbs 3:5

Some years ago I had to face the fact that although I said, "I trust God," my mind proved that I really didn't. I wanted to trust Him, but the truth was that I worried and felt fearful and anxious in many situations. Being truthful with myself helped me to begin dealing with the negative mental habits that were hindering my faith. I can't say that I am totally worry free at this point in my life, but I have come a long way toward the goal, and the less I worry, the less stress I have! There is no doubt that our thoughts and our stress levels are closely connected.

Through various articles I have read over the years, I have learned that stress and worry can affect our physical and emotional health in many ways. Physically, it can affect the nervous system and cause a variety of problems; it can also affect the musculoskeletal system, causing headaches and muscle tension. The respiratory system can be adversely affected, causing hyperventilation that can lead to panic attacks. Stress can also affect the cardiovascular system (increased heart rate, artery inflammation), the endocrine system (excess stress hormones released), the gastrointestinal system (acid reflux, stomach ulcers, constipation, irritable bowel syndrome/diarrhea), and the reproductive system (lower sperm production, absent/irregular menstrual cycle). Emotionally, it can cause anxiety, depression, sleep deprivation, and more.

When we worry, we are searching for answers to our problems, hoping we will find a way to control situations in our life, but the truth is that we were never in control anyway, because God is. Instead of using our power to attempt to control situations and people, we should use it to control ourselves. Instead of worrying about things we cannot control, we should control our worry!

> Instead of worrying about things we cannot control, we should control our worry!

We will never lower our stress levels unless we learn to think properly. By properly, I mean believing the best while trusting God to take care of our problems.

We can make any problem worse by worrying about it!

It is not God's will that we live under the pressure of stress, and He has provided a way for us to avoid most of it.

> Do not let your hearts be troubled (distressed, agitated). You believe in and adhere to and trust in and rely on God; believe in and adhere to and trust in and rely also on Me.
>
> John 14:1

> Peace I leave with you; My [own] peace I now give and bequeath to you. Not as the world gives do I give to you. Do not let your hearts be troubled, neither let them be afraid. [Stop allowing yourselves to be agitated and disturbed; and do not permit yourselves to be fearful and intimidated and cowardly and unsettled.]
>
> John 14:27

Do not be anxious about anything, but in every situation, by prayer and petition, with thanksgiving, present your requests to God. And the peace of God, which transcends all understanding, will guard your hearts and your minds in Christ Jesus.

Philippians 4:6-7 (NIV)

There was a time in my life when I would have read these scripture verses and thought, *I wish I could do that when I have a problem, but I am just a worrier.* But now I know that God didn't create me as a worrier, and since He has instructed me not to worry, there must be a way for me to avoid it! And here we run into the same principle I have been presenting throughout the book—to avoid worry, we must choose to think positively on purpose. If we are passive in troubled times, our minds will be filled with worry, fear, and anxiety, but we can choose to avoid the stress of those power-draining habits by *deciding* how we are going to think!

Lean on God

It is very important to remember to always lean on God and ask for His grace (strength, ability) to help you do whatever needs to be done. When it comes to renewing our minds and learning to think the way God thinks, I can tell you that mere "trying" in our own strength won't work. We need God's help every step of the way. He has equipped us with the "mind of Christ" (see 1 Corinthians 2:16). He has made right thinking possible for us, but we still need His help. God wants us to be totally dependent on Him rather than being independent. He is waiting to help you— just ask!

Stop Upsetting Yourself!

To *upset* is to make unhappy, disappointed, or worried. It is also described by words like *unsettle*, *disquiet*, *perturb*, *bother*, *agitate*, *fluster*, *ruffle*, and *unnerve*. I can't imagine that any one of us would want to do this to ourselves, and yet that is exactly what we do when we choose to worry. Worry is meditating (thinking) about your problem over and over. While it may be wise to think through your situation and ponder if there is any action you should take to make things better, it is unwise to let the problem sit on your mind like a heavy weight for days at a time, interfering with good thoughts you could be thinking about.

The more we worry, the more tension we experience, and the more emotionally distraught and upset we feel. Our thoughts affect our emotions, and we can upset ourselves or calm ourselves down by what we choose to think about. If I continually think about the wrong things, I can get so upset that I feel as if I may scream! Some people say, "I feel like I am losing my mind," and that is exactly what they have done. They have given up the control of their thoughts to an enemy who is bent on killing, stealing, and destroying (see John 10:10).

The main thing we must comprehend is that worry is a complete waste of time and energy. It creates stress in our bodies, and long-term stress has unbelievably destructive side effects.

When we feel emotionally upset, we can calm ourselves down by choosing to think on something other than our problems. Invite a friend who is a positive person to lunch, listen to some happy and comforting music, or go do something for someone else in need. I have found that reading material on the effects of stress may also be helpful. When we remind ourselves of the long-term results of our actions, it may help us be wise enough to make a change in how we approach life before serious damage is done.

I Want Some Peace

For a large part of my life, I had no idea what stress was doing to me, but I found out when I finally started having serious physical problems. I was working too hard and had done so for too long. I wasn't sleeping enough, and I wasn't saying no to people when I really needed to. My life was out of balance!

I kept praying for peace and thinking that if people and circumstances would just change, then I could have it. I finally learned that I was the one who needed to change and that it really wasn't "my life" that was stealing my peace, but I was giving it up through wrong thoughts and reactions. My blood pressure was high, I had back and neck pain from tension, daily headaches, acid reflux, constipation, problems sleeping, and eventually an inability to relax the muscles in my body, which ultimately drove me to seek some answers.

Like most of us, I wanted an easy fix, so I went to doctors hoping for a magic pill to swallow once a day that would solve my problems. However, I became even more upset when the doctors told me that although my symptoms were very real, the root cause of my problems was stress. I actually got angry when they told me that, because I viewed stress as me not being able to handle life. I had convinced myself that I was strong and in control and that the doctors just didn't know what the problem was, so they excused it away with the "stress diagnosis" that so many people hear.

As I continued to have more and more problems, God finally

got through to me by putting material in my hands that really helped me understand what stress was and how to begin eliminating it. I had to make several lifestyle changes, and if you are stressed to the point that it is becoming a problem, you will need to do the same thing.

Jesus said that when we are worn out and overburdened, our first response should be to come to Him!

> Jesus said that when we are worn out and overburdened, our first response should be to come to Him!

> Come to me, all you who are weary and burdened, and I will give you rest. Take my yoke upon you and learn from me, for I am gentle and humble in heart, and you will find rest for your souls. For my yoke is easy and my burden is light.
>
> Matthew 11:28–30 (NIV)

Come to Jesus, talk openly with Him about the way you are feeling, and ask Him to reveal to you the changes you need to make in order to begin to heal. They say that only a fool thinks he can keep doing the same thing and get a different result. Prayer doesn't always result in a miraculous delivery from our problems. More often than not, it results in God giving us wisdom and revealing what we need to do (with His help) to effect a positive change.

I like this short story that shows what a waste worry is:

> J. Arthur Rank, an English executive, decided to do all his worrying on one day each week. He chose Wednesdays. When anything happened that gave him anxiety and annoyed his ulcer, he would write it down and put it in his worry box and forget about it until next Wednesday.

The interesting thing was that on the following Wednesday when he opened his worry box, he found that most of the things that had disturbed him the past six days were already settled. It would have been useless to have worried about them.[1]

Once when I went to Jesus about the stress I was feeling, He said, "Joyce, you think too much." I do have a busy mind and tend to think about things that if left alone would work themselves out.

As I have had my "come to Jesus" meetings, I have received many simple but stress-relieving ideas from Him. For example:

- Change my schedule and leave margin in it so I don't end up rushing from thing to thing with no breaks in between.
- Take time to do things I enjoy instead of being excessive about work, because no matter how long I work, there will always be another project that needs to be done.
- Have a plan, but don't get upset if my plan is interrupted for valid reasons.
- Make better choices about what I eat, because it is true that the kind of fuel I put into my body will determine how well it functions for me.
- Have a regular bedtime and get good sleep.
- Don't try to keep all the people happy all the time at the cost of living with unhealthy stress.
- Say no when I need to!

These are only a few of the helpful things I have learned and now practice daily, but as you can see, they are all fairly simple things. Let me say again that the first thing to do when you are ready for help is come to Jesus. He will guide and direct you into a healthy lifestyle.

Worry Causes Untimely Death

Christy Henrich was a talented American teenager who was one of the country's best gymnasts. When she tried out for the Olympic team in 1988, a judge told her she was too fat—Christy was four feet eleven inches and weighed only ninety-five pounds.

Upon hearing the critique of the judge, Christy began starving herself. Some days she ate only a slice of an apple. And if she ate more than that, she would force herself to vomit so as not to gain any weight.

Though she missed out on qualifying for the Olympic team that year, Christy placed fourth in the uneven parallel bars in the World Championships just a year later. However, Christy's story doesn't have a happy ending. Tragically, Christy Henrich died at the young age of twenty-two in a Kansas City hospital. Her organs failed—she weighed only fifty-two pounds.[2]

One of the things that people, and women in particular, worry about is how much they weigh, and how they look. Although we do want to maintain a normal weight and present ourselves in a pleasing way, we cannot all be stick-thin and look as if we are the one person on the planet that is free from the aging process. Do the best you can, but don't worry about weight and appearance. Make peace with the parts of your body that you don't care for and learn to downplay them while making the most of your strong points.

For example, if you don't like the shape of your nose, then make sure you have a stunning hairstyle. If you don't like the way your legs look, then don't wear shorts. Worrying won't change a thing about the way we look! Most of us would not go to the extremes that Christy Henrich did and actually suffer an untimely death, but we may be shortening our life span by worrying excessively about many things, including our weight and appearance.

I am recommending that you stop worrying and thinking excessively about weight if that is a problem for you. If you eat right, you will eventually weigh what you are supposed to weigh. It may not be what your skinny friend weighs, but whatever it is, learn to embrace it and stop worrying. Worry never made anyone skinny, but there are lots of people who eat when they are stressed, so it may be adding to your problem instead of solving it.

Make a list of things you worry about and pray over it daily, asking God to help you cast your care on Him in each of the areas. As situations come up in your life that would normally cause you to worry, choose to think differently than you have in the past.

Stress can be a positive force that helps us perform well in a sport or at a job interview. Faced with challenges or even danger, the body kicks into gear: Hormones flood in that elevate our heart rate, increase blood pressure, boost energy, and prepare us for action. The experts call it the "fight or flight" response, but when we get stuck in that mode, it can have serious consequences on our health. The longer the stress lasts, the worse it is for both your mind and body. God has created us to be able to handle normal amounts of stress, but when we begin to feel tension from it, especially when it is chronic, it is time to take action. God has given us the amazing gift of life, and we should value it enough to protect it.

The Tension Trigger

Learn to recognize tension and let that be a trigger, or a signal to purposely relax. I spend a lot of time writing, and the stress of deep thought while simultaneously putting those thoughts on the computer, combined with sitting in the same position for hours at a time can definitely cause tension. My neck and shoulders will begin to mildly ache, and if I ignore that signal, they eventually move into pain, and I start to feel exhausted. If I will get up at the first sign of tension, take a short break of even two to five minutes, and stretch a little, it relieves the stress, and I can go back to work.

When I am discussing something with someone, and we are getting into a heated disagreement, I can feel the tension as every muscle in my body starts to stiffen. I have learned to let that be a trigger or a signal to either stop talking or take the conversation in another direction. If I am rushing from thing to thing, I may start to feel tense or overwhelmed, and that is a trigger for me to slow down.

We all have these little signs that show up in our body, letting us know that we are on overload, but we have to learn to respect them. Sometimes I call them "warnings." They are like storm sirens that go off, letting us know that a storm is coming. For some, it may be shortness of breath, a headache, an upset stomach, or sweating, but whatever it is, learn to recognize your warning signs and respect them enough to make appropriate changes.

The Value of Solitude

One of the things we lack in our society is solitude. We live in a noisy, high-pressure, busy world, where more is expected of most of us than we can possibly do. The world more than likely won't change, but we can. One of the main things that combats and offsets stress is solitude. I absolutely love quiet times!!!! But there was a time when I became restless if things got quiet, because I was addicted to noise and activity. I have discovered that even five minutes of quiet and solitude can restore my soul to a restful place and relieve stress. It gives me time to actually breathe deeply and do nothing.

If we scheduled more solitude and quiet time for ourselves, we would probably be able to schedule fewer doctor appointments. If you are like I was, you may have to build up an ability to be quiet. If it is difficult for you, then start with a few minutes three or four times a day and gradually increase your tolerance level. My favorite times of the day, and the ones that strengthen me most, are in the morning before anyone else wakes up, and at night after everyone else has gone to bed. It isn't that I don't enjoy people, because I enjoy them very much, but some quiet time in the morning helps me get ready to be with them, and quiet time in the evening helps me recover from being with them. As we all know, not all people are easy to get along with, and since we never know what a day may bring, it is best to be spiritually ready!

> I never found the companion that was so companionable as solitude.
>
> Henry David Thoreau, *Walden*

We tend to think that our existence is only justified when we are *doing* something, but that is not true. We are human *beings*, not human *doings*! God doesn't love us more when we are doing something than He does when are enjoying quiet. Our busyness makes us feel important, but it doesn't make us more important to God.

I finally had to face the truth that I felt more acceptable when I was working than at any other time. Some of that came from my abusive childhood, some of it from my strong, work-oriented temperament, but neither could be an excuse to not change. Whatever the reason was, the result was the same. Too much activity without any solitude was damaging my future and preventing me from enjoying the present. Let me stop and say "Thank You" to my Heavenly Father for revealing to me that He had not created me merely to "do," but also to "be."

Think About It!

- Your thoughts and your stress levels are closely related.
- Worry just makes a problem worse. Believe the best, and trust God to take care of every situation.
- To avoid stress and worry, choose to think positive thoughts on purpose.
- The first thing to do when you are ready for help is come to Jesus. He will guide and direct you into a healthy lifestyle.
- Make a list of the things that worry you and pray over that list daily. Cast your care upon the Lord.

CHAPTER 15

The Mind-Body Connection

There is no question that the things we think have a tremendous effect upon our bodies. If we can change our thinking, the body frequently heals itself.

C. Everett Coop, MD

Our bodies are like automobiles that God provides for us to drive around earth in. If we want them to perform to their maximum ability and be around for a long time, then we need to choose to think in ways that will help them. All of our thoughts, good or bad, have an effect on our physical being. The mind and body are definitely connected.

Today I am spending the day with a close friend whom I don't get to see very often, and I am really looking forward to it. All of my thoughts are happy ones, and I have noticed that I feel better physically than I have in a few days. I didn't necessarily feel bad previously, but today I feel great! My energy level is up, and I feel strong. I have also been dealing with a minor health problem that has been lingering for eight weeks, but nobody has been able to provide an accurate diagnosis or prescribe anything to make it better. Last night, I encountered a new symptom that shed light on what the problem is, and I now know what to do to get well. That has replaced reasoning and concern with hope, and it has also increased my energy.

Positive, hopeful thoughts increase energy, whereas negative, hopeless ones drain energy. Physical tiredness is not always

Positive, hopeful thoughts increase energy, whereas negative, hopeless ones drain energy.

the result of wrong thinking. We certainly can have a sickness or disease that leads to loss of energy, or we may even wake up tired for no known reason. I had the stomach flu for three days last week and I felt terrible. I was tired and weak, and it wasn't caused from wrong thinking. Things don't always happen for the same reason, but I do know, and science and medical technology verify, that the mind and body have a close connection and that our thinking does have a direct effect on our body.

Dr. Caroline Leaf has written extensively on this topic. In her book *Switch On Your Brain*, she states:

> Research shows that 75 to 98 percent of mental, physical, and behavioral illness comes from one's thought life. This staggering and eye-opening statistic means only 2 to 25 percent of mental and physical illnesses come from the environment and genes....
>
> We may have a fixed set of genes in our chromosomes, but which of those genes are active and *how* they are active has a great deal to do with how we think and process our experiences. Our thoughts produce words and behaviors, which in turn stimulate more thinking and choices that build more thoughts in an endless cycle.
>
> We are constantly reacting to circumstances and events, and as this cycle goes on, our brains become shaped by the process in either a positive, good-quality-of-life direction or a negative, toxic, poor-quality-of-life direction.

So it is the quality of our thinking and choices (consciousness) and our reactions that determine our "brain architecture"—the shape or design of the brain and *resultant* quality of the health of our minds and bodies.

Science and Scripture both show that we are wired for love and optimism and so when we react by thinking negatively and making negative choices, the quality of our thinking suffers, which means the quality of our brain architecture suffers. It is comforting—and challenging— to know that negative thinking is not the norm....

Toxic thinking wears down the brain.

The Institute of HeartMath, an internationally recognized, nonprofit research organization that helps people reduce stress, discusses an experiment titled "Local and Nonlocal Effects of Coherent Heart Frequencies on Conformational Changes of DNA." This study showed that thinking and feeling anger, fear, and frustration caused DNA to change shape according to thoughts and feelings. The DNA responded by tightening up and becoming shorter, switching off many DNA codes, which reduced quality expression. So we feel shut down by negative emotions, and our body feels this too. But here's the great part: the negative shutdown or poor quality of the DNA codes was *reversed* by feelings of love, joy, appreciation, and gratitude! The researchers also found that HIV positive patients who had positive thoughts and feelings had 300,000 times more resistance to the disease than those without positive feelings. So the takeaway here is that when we operate in our normal love design— which is being made in God's image (Gen. 1:26)—we are able to change the shape of our DNA for the better.

So when we make a poor-quality decision—when we choose to engage toxic thoughts (for example, unforgiveness, bitterness, irritation, or feelings of not coping)—we change the DNA and subsequent genetic expression, which then changes the shape of our brain wiring in a negative direction. This immediately puts the brain into protection mode, and the brain translates these poor-quality, toxic thoughts as negative stress. This stress then manifests in our bodies. But the most exciting part of this study was the hope it demonstrated because the positive attitude, the good choice, rewired everything back to the original healthy positive state. These scientists basically proved we can renew our minds....

[Here are two powerful statistics confirming that much] of mental and physical illness comes from one's thought life:

- A study by the American Medical Association found that stress is a factor in 75 percent of all illnesses and diseases that people suffer from today.
- The association between stress and disease is a colossal 85 percent.

The main point of this [information] is that mind controls matter. If we get this right, we have enormous potential to reach peak health. If we get it wrong, we will be our own worst enemies.[1]

Positive Thoughts Improve Health

Many years ago a woman shared with me her experience of receiving healing from arthritis, and it is quite amazing. She had been suffering greatly for several years with painful arthritis in several joints of her body. Medicine helped some, but nothing brought any true healing until she heard teaching on the devastating effects of bitterness and unresolved anger. She had been hurt deeply by her mother and literally hated her. The thoughts she meditated on frequently about her mother were negatively affecting her in ways she was totally unaware of.

Through the teaching of Jesus on the need to forgive our enemies, she found the grace to do so, and over the next few months she noticed that her pain from arthritis was gradually disappearing. The swelling and stiffness in her joints was diminishing and continued to do so until she was completely healed. I am not suggesting that everyone with arthritis is filled with bitterness, but in this case she was, and the healing she sought could not come until she was free from it.

More and more studies are proving that the physical body responds negatively to negative thinking and it responds positively to positive thinking. Every part of the human body has a critical role to play, and if one part is functioning in any unhealthy way, then the entire body can often suffer the consequences; it is the same when a part of the body is functioning in a healthy manner.

Recently, I read a story about a man named Ed: Ed remembers having an upset stomach when he was a child and his grandmother asking him if he was having a problem at school. What she knew instinctively we are at last beginning to prove scientifically: that there is an intimate and dynamic relationship between what is going on with our feelings and thoughts and what happens in the body.

A *TIME* magazine special showed that happiness, hopefulness, optimism, and contentment "appear to reduce the risk or limit the severity of cardiovascular disease, pulmonary disease, diabetes, hypertension, colds and upper-respiratory infections," while "depression—the extreme opposite of happiness—can worsen heart disease, diabetes and a host of other illnesses."[2]

Examining Negative Thoughts and Emotions

When you are irritated or frustrated, where do you experience those feelings in your body? When you are late for an appointment, does your stomach start to hurt or feel upset? Do your muscles become tense when you have to wait in a long line and nobody is in a rush but you? When you hear that someone you trusted has told your secret, do you experience shortness of breath as you become more and more anxious? What happens in your body when you become anxious or angry? Have you ever really paid attention to how you feel physically when you are experiencing negative thoughts and emotions? If not, it could be an educational process in which you might learn a lot. What happens to your heart rate? Do you get pain in your head or neck, or do you begin to sweat?

I have observed that when I have something on my mind that is pressuring me, I don't sleep as well as I normally do and then I feel tired the next day. I really don't like it when someone gives me a problem at night and there is no way for me to solve it until the next day. I like to deal with troubling issues right away and get them off my mind. The apostle Paul tells us not to let the sun set on our anger (see Ephesians 4:26), and I think it best not to let it set on our worries either.

Memories

Pay attention to how memories affect you. If I let my mind drift back to specific instances when my father was abusing me or beating my mother, or yelling in anger, or the fear I experienced constantly throughout my childhood, my body responds with tightness and I clench my teeth. I don't allow myself to do that very often, but there are occasions when I find my mind has gone to a wrong memory, and I have to retrieve it quickly before it traps me in a painful place that is unhealthy. Good memories have the opposite effect. They produce peace and relaxation, both of which cooperate with the healing properties God has placed in our bodies.

If I allow my thoughts today to be on what went wrong yesterday or mistakes I may have made, it will only zap my strength for today. No wonder the apostle Paul said that one of his greatest aspirations was to forget what was behind him and to press toward the future (see Philippians 3:12–14). Perhaps he knew two thousand years ago what we are finding out today. Over and over, God's Word instructs us to remember the good things that God has done for us. I suspect that God also knew what the scientist and chemists are just discovering about how thoughts affect the rest of our lives. God sure is smart, and it is a shame that more people don't listen to Him and believe what He says! I always chuckle when a "scientific discovery" reveals something God revealed in His Word centuries ago.

Let's look at a few examples of this in God's Word:

God told the Israelites to *remember* that they were once slaves in Egypt, and how He redeemed and delivered them (see Deuteronomy 24:18). I am sure when they were delivered, it was an extremely joyous occasion, and remembering it often would surely help them in many ways.

Esther put her life on the line when she went before King Ahasuerus without being summoned to plead for the lives of the Israelites whom Haman secretly planned to destroy. When her plan worked and they were all saved, the people took it upon themselves to keep a two-day feast every year to *remember* what God had done for them (see Esther 9:27–29).

When David was dealing with depression, he purposely *remembered* a time when he led the people with shouting and praise (see Psalm 42:4–5). I am sure that David was applying the principle I am suggesting. He was thinking about things that made him happy to help get rid of the depression he was experiencing.

David found the key to satisfaction. He said:

> My whole being shall be satisfied as with marrow and fatness; and my mouth shall praise You with joyful lips.
>
> When I remember You upon my bed and meditate on You in the night watches.
>
> For You have been my help, and in the shadow of Your wings will I rejoice.
>
> Psalm 63:5–7

There are many instances recorded in the Bible when God instructed His people to remember, recount, and recall His mighty acts and the things He had done for them. When they failed to do so, they lost their appreciation, became selfish and independent, and always went back into bondage. Remembering the good things in life is certainly helpful and keeps us on the happy path of gratitude. The simple fact is that thankful people are happy people, and happy people are often healthier than sad, discouraged, hopeless, and depressed people.

The mind-body connection is now a proven fact, and it gives us an easy and inexpensive way to help maintain good health. Anybody can think positive, good thoughts if they will choose to do so.

I love that I can improve my health by thinking better thoughts. Nobody wants to be a victim, and we certainly don't want to be victimized by our thoughts. Learning to think purposely and aggressively, instead of passively providing an empty space for chance or the devil to fill, is the way to become the victor instead of the victim. Ask God to help you, and get started today on your way to a healthier mind and body.

Think About It!

- Positive, hopeful thoughts increase your energy levels.
- Confront troubling issues right away. Deal with them, refusing to let worry affect your spirit, soul, and body.
- Instead of focusing on what is wrong, set your mind on what is right—the good things God has done in your life.
- Thankful people are happy people, and happy people are healthier people.

CHAPTER 16

The Mind-Performance Connection

All things are ready, if our minds be so.
William Shakespeare, *Henry V*

Learning about the mind-body connection won't necessarily cure all of our illnesses and turn us into superheroes, but we can improve our lives in many ways by learning how to think properly. Not only does the mind affect our bodies, but it also affects our performance in all areas of life. If you are going for a job interview, I am sure that you want to perform well and appear to be confident and capable. No company wants to hire anyone who has no confidence that they can do the job they are applying for. The thoughts you think prior to the interview will determine, at least in large part, how you perform during the interview.

If a person fears failure and they go to the interview doubting they will get the job and entertaining all sorts of thoughts that minimize their ability, they surely will not get the job. Here are two different ways Brian might think if he were going on a job interview:

- **Option 1**—For days prior to the interview, Brian thinks, *I doubt they will hire me. I rarely win at anything. I am shy and lack confidence, and I am afraid they will notice it. I was laid off from* *my last job, and they said it was nothing personal, just company-wide cutbacks, but I know they just didn't like me. I am so nervous; I hope I don't shake in front of the interviewer.*

If these are Brian's thoughts, they will also come out in conversation and do even more damage than the thoughts alone would. When he goes to the interview, he will perform precisely according to the way his thoughts have prepared him to perform. Brian won't get the job!

- **Option 2**—For days prior to the interview, Brian thinks, *I believe God will give me favor when I go to this interview and that I will get this job. I am confident in God. I believe He is with me at all times and that He enables me to perform any task I need to perform. I am a hard worker and am always willing to learn. I look forward to this interview, and I definitely believe that if this is the right job for me, then I will get it!*

  If these are Brian's thoughts, he will enter the interview with his head up and a smile on his face. He will look the interviewer in the eye and not let his gaze shift from side to side due to fear and insecurity. He will answer the questions honestly and calmly. He will sincerely convey that he would love to have the job and is ready to work hard and learn. The person interviewing Brian will sense his confidence and sincerity, and he will definitely be one of the people they will strongly consider for the position.

William Shakespeare said, "All things are ready, if our minds be so."[1] A job is ready for Brian somewhere, but his mind must be ready to have it! Success waits for all of us, but we will never have it if we think of how we may fail.

> *Success waits for all of us, but we will never have it if we think of how we may fail.*

Here are a few quotes to meditate on that I found to be helpful:

> You have to expect things of yourself before you can do them.
>
> Michael Jordan[2]

> I have learned that your mind can amaze your body if you just keep telling yourself, I can do it…I can do it… I can do it.
>
> Jon Erickson[3]

> Never let the fear of striking out get in your way.
>
> Babe Ruth[4]

> Sometimes the biggest problem is in your head. You've got to believe you can play a shot instead of wondering where your next bad shot is coming from.
>
> Jack Nicklaus[5]

> The most important part of a player's body is above his shoulders.
>
> Ty Cobb[6]

Each of the people quoted above is an athlete. They have learned that they cannot be successful in their sport if they are unable to control their thoughts. Successful performance requires successful thinking!

In order to perform successfully, an athlete must train his mind and his body. He must have the ability to stay focused under pressure and not allow fearful, self-defeating thoughts to fill his head. If a batter in a baseball game hears the umpire yell, "Strike one!" he cannot think, *I am afraid I will strike out.* He must believe that he will succeed the next time he swings. Even if he ends up striking out, he should think, *I will get a hit the next time I am at bat.*

An overly religious individual who tends to be judgmental might say, "Joyce, you are merely teaching 'mind control,' and I think we just need to trust God!" Certainly I believe we must trust God, but the truth is that we can also make the choice to control our minds so our thoughts go in line with God's will. We are partners with God in life and we can follow the guidelines He has set forth in His Word. One of those guidelines is that we learn to think as He does, so we can be and have what He desires!

We certainly cannot control all of our performance and reactions to things by thinking in certain ways. God is ultimately in control, and we succeed by leaning on and trusting in Him, and not merely through positive thinking. However, there is nothing in any kind of negative thinking that would help us in any way. Even if I were a ballplayer (which I am not), and I thought I would hit a home run but ended up striking out, at least I wouldn't have drained my energy for the next opportunity through defeatist, energy-draining mental habits.

Think About What You Want, Not What You Have

Surely, as Moses led the Israelites through the wilderness toward the Promised Land, he was thinking of what they could have, not what they had previously had. Before God delivered them, they were oppressed as slaves in Egypt and had been sorely mistreated.

But as they journeyed to a better place, one of the very bad habits they had was becoming discouraged during hard times and

> Your life cannot go forward
> if your mind is going
> backward!

thinking about the few pitiful things
they did have as slaves. Your life cannot go forward if your mind is going
backward!

> If they had been thinking with [homesick] remembrance of
> that country from which they were emigrants, they would
> have found constant opportunity to return to it.
>
> Hebrews 11:15

Look forward in your thinking. Get your mind off your failures
and disappointments, because there is a victory waiting for you!
Any great athlete has developed the ability to think about the next
successful play he is expecting and not the unsuccessful one he just
had. He may examine his less than stellar performance in order to
learn from it, but he doesn't have to wallow in the negativity of it.

You may not be an athlete, but you do want to perform well
at whatever you are doing, and the principles of how the mind
affects our performance in all areas of life are basically the same.

Strength Training

In order for me to perform at an optimum level, I have discovered
that I need to work out and exercise regularly. I know some of
you may cringe when I say "exercise," but you can relax, because
I am not going to try to convince you to exercise. I do think it is
beneficial for everyone, but in this instance I want to draw out
one principle I am learning about how my mind affects my performance during my training sessions.

I have been working out regularly with a trainer for ten years, because I want to be as strong as I can for the work God has called me to do. It was difficult in the beginning to keep going, because I had never exercised and everything I did made me extremely sore (sometimes painfully sore). I am not exaggerating when I say that I believe I was sore someplace on my body for two years. Quite often people have a goal, but when they experience inconvenience, discomfort, or sacrifice, they go backward instead of continuing to go forward. I had to learn to believe that I could do the exercises I was being given, and it amazed me to learn how quickly our bodies will adapt to doing new things that we have never done before. I am easily doing exercises now that a few years ago made me laugh in disbelief when my trainer first described them to me. I have learned not to think and say, "I can't do that," but to replace that self-defeating thought with an enabling one. Now I think, *I can learn to do that.* My performance is enhanced by how I think!

One of the things my trainer told me over and over was to focus my mind on the muscle I was working on. He said that I would actually get more benefit from it if I did. I had difficulty learning to do this, because my mind is often on something else. I do most things fast and exercise was no different, but I was continually told that I needed to slow down and focus if I wanted to get full value out of my efforts. I have finally gotten much better at that part, but am still working on focusing on the muscle I am working on. No matter what we are doing, focus is required in order to have optimum performance. We have to control our thoughts, because thoughts affect performance. When we discipline ourselves to focus on what we are doing, we perform with a greater

> *No matter what we are doing, focus is required in order to have optimum performance.*

degree of accuracy and excellence. Focus actually helps release the strength that we have, and focus is simply directing your thoughts to what you are currently doing.

Performing well is not merely a matter of desire, but it also requires discipline. There is no shortage of people who start things. They are zealous when they begin but lack the discipline to keep at it until they get the desired result. They have big ideas, but not enough disciplined focus to follow through. Dave and I know a man who owns and operates a gym. People pay a monthly or yearly fee to join and they can work out as often as they want to. Most of the people are on an autopay plan. Their fee is taken directly from their bank account or placed on their credit card. He told me that out of all the people who sign up and pay regularly, only 40 percent of them show up to exercise.

One might wonder why they keep paying the fee if they are not going to go to the gym. I think it is because it makes them feel better to think they may go, or to plan to go, even if they never actually do it. *Tomorrow* may be one of the most dangerous words in the English language. We comfort ourselves in our lack of discipline by promising to do it tomorrow! Today we think we will go tomorrow, but when tomorrow comes, we dread going and put it off one more day.

One of the reasons why we often don't follow through and complete what we start is because we find it to be more difficult than we had imagined it would be. The more you do anything, the easier it will become. God has given us an amazing ability to adapt to new things. For example: A new employee who is hired for the road crew may find the travel very tiring and difficult in the beginning, but after a while, it becomes part of their normal routine, and if they stay home too long, they are anxious to get back on the road. If you are in the midst of doing something that is fairly new for you and finding it difficult, I urge you to give it time before you give up. If we give up too quickly, we often miss out on some of the best things in life.

Dread and Performance

Thoughts that make us dread doing something we need to do are self-defeating. I won't allow myself to dread going to the gym. I am committed to going, so why should I make myself miserable by dreading what I already know I am going to do? I won't allow myself to dread even the most mundane things I have to do, simply because I know that if I dread them, they will be difficult for me to do with a good attitude.

How many things do you dread doing that you know you have to do anyway? Possibly more than you realize, and by dreading them, you are negatively affecting your ability to perform, as well as your ability to enjoy what you do. When you dread doing a thing, all the natural skills you use to perform the task are hindered through wrong thinking. Our thoughts can aid us in our performance or they can hinder us, and it is up to us which one it will be.

Instead of dreading any task that is before you, why not think like this: *This is something I need to do, and I can do, and I am going to do it with a good attitude. I refuse to dread daily tasks, and I am not going to allow wrong thinking to rob me of my ability to perform strong and well.* People often announce to anyone who will listen all of the things they are dreading.

"I dread cleaning my house." "I dread driving in traffic every morning and night as I go back and forth from my job." "I dread going to work because I hate my job." "I dread going to the dentist" (well, maybe you can dread that). The list is endless concerning things we can either dread or choose to approach with a mental attitude that will actually help us.

Think *I can* thoughts, not *I can't* thoughts.

Think *I love* thoughts, not *I hate* thoughts.

Think *I look forward to* thoughts, not *I resent* thoughts.

Now is the time to think better so you can perform better. Get the most out of your skills and talents. God has given them to you, and you can glorify Him with them by performing at optimum levels.

Think About It!

- Not only does the mind affect our bodies, but it also affects our performance in all areas of life.
- Success waits for all of us, but we will never have it if we think of how we may fail.
- Replace self-defeating thoughts with enabling thoughts in order to perform at your highest level.
- Performing well is not solely a matter of desire, but also discipline.
- If we give up too quickly, we often miss out on some of the best things in life.

CHAPTER 17

Where Did All My Energy Go?

Goals help you channel your energy into action.

Les Brown

I believe that God gives each of us abilities and corresponding energy that will help us fulfill our destiny. We aren't born tired and listless. A new baby seems to want to do something and go someplace from the time they are born. If they were listless and had no energy, we would take them to the doctor. If you are lacking energy, you should look for the root of the problem! Many of us behave as if our get-up-and-go has got up and gone. When that happens, I believe it can be due to faulty thinking in some area of our life. We might be going through a season in which we are tired of what we are doing, but that is not an indication that we are to begin doing it in a halfhearted way. One day last week I was especially tired physically and not controlling my thoughts as well as I should have, and I thought of retirement! I took a day off and the next day I thought, *What do I think I would do with myself if I retired? I LOVE WHAT I AM DOING!* It is important not to overreact to emotions because they may fall one day and rise up the next.

We all get tired of what we are doing at times. Moms get tired of taking care of kids, cleaning house, and cooking. The office clerk gets tired of her job, and the president of the corporation gets tired of having so much responsibility all the time. Kids get tired of going to school, and they get tired of being kids. They want to grow up and run their own lives, while adults often wish they could have fewer decisions to make and be more childlike. People in the public eye want more privacy and they long to be *normal*, and normal people want to be well known and recognized in public.

The only people who succeed in life are those who can do what they know is important with or without emotional excitement to motivate them! When your get-up-and-go has got up and gone, you need to get up and get it back. We won't become so tired of doing what we do in life if we are more careful concerning how we think about our lives. The more appreciative I am for the life I have, the more I enjoy living it.

> When your get-up-and-go has got up and gone, you need to get up and get it back.

I recently heard of a man who had to be released from his job, and it was not due to being unskilled. He was, in fact, very qualified for the position, and he had worked at the company for several years, but he had grown unappreciative and developed an attitude of entitlement. His thinking was full of what he thought he should be getting that he wasn't getting and how much better a job he could do if he were the department manager instead of the man who had the position. He thought he was being overlooked and mistreated, and it filled his heart with strife and bitterness. The truth was that he had a very good job with great benefits.

Hopefully, he will learn from this experience and realize that his negative thinking influenced his attitude and behavior. If he can face the truth, then he won't have to keep making the same mistake over and over throughout his life. All too often people like this go through life blaming others for all their disappointments, and they are never able to change because they never take responsibility for their actions. It is initially less painful to lash out at someone else than it is to do some serious soul searching and face the truth.

He may have believed that his thoughts were private and nobody knew how he felt, but the exact opposite was true. What is in our hearts does come out of our mouths and shows up in our attitudes and behaviors. He regularly insinuated that the department manager was not doing a good job. A lack of gratitude on his part resulted in loss of zeal and enthusiasm regarding his job. Instead of doing the excellent job that he once did, he was doing a mediocre job at best. These types of situations are very sad to me. I see the capabilities in people and so desperately wish they could see how their thoughts, words, attitudes, and behaviors can either release or imprison those capabilities.

I urge you to be careful about the kind of thoughts you allow to roll around in your mind when you find yourself getting a little tired of doing what you do. Stay positive and if you should come to the point, after a reasonable amount of time has passed, that you are confident that you need to make a change, then do so. But don't blame other people and leave with a bitter, resentful attitude.

There are times in life when God lets us know a change is ahead for us by removing the desire we once had to do what we are doing. It is very wise to give these feelings the "time test" to be sure they are not mere emotions that would lead to regret if acted upon. If they pass the test and remain for a long time, it may be safe to assume that you need to prayerfully consider a change.

A master builder went to his boss and said, "I'm too tired to build any more houses. I've decided to retire." A few days later the contractor met with Clyde, the master builder, and said, "Please. Would you reconsider and build one final house? I really need you to head up this project. Please."

After thinking about it, the carpenter agreed and began working on his last project. However, his heart wasn't in it. As a result, the workmanship was shoddy and the quality fell far below his usual standards. The house barely passed inspection.

On the last day of the project, the contractor gathered his employees together at the job site [and] asked the carpenter and his wife to be present. The boss announced, "As you know, this is Clyde's last day with us. He has been a faithful employee of our company for years and we want to do something special to honor him. Clyde, this house you have built is not going to be sold. We are giving it to you and your wife as a gift for your years of service. This is your retirement home—one I know you will enjoy for the rest of your life."[1]

Clyde let his zeal fade away, and I am sure that during the building of this last house his thoughts might have been *This is my last project and I am quitting after that, so I can slack off and just do anything to get it over with*. If we don't give our all on every project, our reward will not satisfy us. I am sure that Clyde regretted the poor job he did on the house he was now living in.

We all love having emotion to motivate us, but emotions are linked to our thoughts and tend to be abundant at some times and yet totally missing at other times. When emotion is gone and energy seems low, the best thing to do is check your thinking and make adjustments where needed, and then stir yourself up rather than waiting passively for a feeling to motivate you.

It is also wise to check your heart to be sure there is no strife in it, because strife in any area will definitely rob you of much needed energy and zest for life. A friend came to me about her husband, saying she was concerned about him because he seemed to have no motivation to do anything. She thought perhaps he was sick, but he refused to see a doctor. This situation persisted for over two years and was quite severe. He seemed depressed, lazy, apathetic, disinterested in family and life in general. The friend and I prayed together about this situation for a few weeks, and our gracious and wonderful God revealed the root of the problem. After he was confronted at his place of employment about his attitude, he realized he had let strife get into his heart during an incident that had occurred over two years prior, and his thinking had declined to the point where it was literally stealing all of his energy, motivation, and desire to do anything. He wept and repented profusely and was immediately relieved of his burden. His energy returned, and his wife is still telling me how different he is.

Fearful Thoughts

Fearful thoughts can also rob us of much-needed energy. Fear that something bad will happen drains us of energy, and faith in God that good things will happen motivates and energizes us.

Timothy, who was a protégé of the apostle Paul, was once actively fulfilling his role in ministry, but his zeal began to fade due to fearful thoughts. There was a great deal of persecution of Christians in his day, and he had probably let his thinking drift into all the bad things that could happen to him if he kept boldly preaching God's Word. His energy was drained through fearful thoughts. Paul told him to "stir himself up in the Lord" by *remembering* the gift of God (the inner fire) given to him at his ordination when Paul and the elders laid hands on him to commission him into ministry (2 Timothy 1:5–6). God had not changed His mind about the call on Timothy's life, but Timothy needed to be encouraged concerning it. Paul also reminded Timothy that God had not given him a spirit of fear but of power, love, and a sound mind (2 Timothy 1:7). God is not the source of fearful thoughts, but Satan is.

God gives us the ability to think soundly. Fear may come against us, but well-informed people know its source and resist it. Courageous people feel the fear and take action anyway. It was time for Timothy to cease behaving according to how he felt, and start taking action on what he knew in his heart.

> Courageous people feel the fear and take action anyway.

We will not be able to keep all fearful thoughts from presenting themselves to our mind, but we certainly don't have to accept them and let them steal our energy, enthusiasm, and zeal.

Timothy's fearful thoughts had to be traded for ones that would help him regain his faith. He had once been a raging fire, and now it seemed he had become cold ashes, but it wasn't too late. All was not lost, because he had the choice to shake off the apathy he was feeling and get up and get going again. Thankfully, Timothy ultimately made decisions based on more than emotion, and he did fulfill the call on his life.

All negative thinking, or any thoughts that might be termed ungodly, steal our energy. Ungodly thoughts would be defined as anything that God's Word teaches us not to do. Things such as angry and vengeful thoughts, as well as bitter and resentful thoughts toward others, would be counterproductive to an energetic life. Jealousy and envy rot the bones, according to Scripture, so they would not help us (see Proverbs 14:30). Greedy and discontented thoughts are not beneficial and should be replaced with thoughts of thanksgiving. Anytime we think bad thoughts, they usually turn into bad words that are spoken by us, and that in turn becomes a bad mood that drains energy. I hope you are beginning to connect the dots, so to speak, and that you are realizing that the root of most problems that people encounter emotionally is directly linked to thoughts they have permitted to fester in their minds.

We can immediately increase our energy level by choosing energy-creating thoughts and meditating on them. It excites me to realize that I may be able to do something about improving my energy level. Admittedly, all loss of energy is not the result of wrong thinking, but even if disease is the source, good thoughts can't do anything but help us.

Guilty and Condemning Thoughts

Some of the most energy-draining types of thoughts are the ones about past mistakes, failure, and sins that produce guilt and condemnation. The devil loves to fill our minds with thoughts of past failures that we cannot do anything about. God, however, offers us complete forgiveness and mercy, as well as a fresh start daily. We choose which way we think. We can think about the past or the future. We can think about what we have lost or the opportunities in front of us. We can think about our sins, or we can think about the goodness and grace of God manifested by sending Jesus to pay for our sins and remove them as far as the East is from the West (see Psalm 103:12).

Guilt is our human effort offered as payment for our sins, but they have already been paid for by the death, bloodshed, and suffering of Jesus. His sacrifice is good once and for all (see Hebrews

> *If Jesus has done it once and for all, then it never needs to be done again.*

9:28, 10:10). Think about the power and finality of that statement! If Jesus has done it once and for all, then it never needs to be done again.

There is nothing we can add to what Jesus has done. We can only humbly and gratefully accept the complete forgiveness He offers and refuse the guilt.

People who love God and want to please Him often suffer terribly with guilty thoughts and feelings over every tiny thing they do wrong, or even think they might have done wrong. I was one of those people, but learning to line my thinking up with God's Word has set me free. When I sin, I am quick to repent, I receive forgiveness, and when guilt comes, I simply think or sometimes say, "I am forgiven completely and there is no guilt or condemnation for those in Christ" (see Romans 8:1). Remember, the mind is the battlefield, and there is no hope of victory and enjoyment of life unless we are willing to learn how to control and properly manage our thoughts and bring them into obedience to Jesus Christ (see 2 Corinthians 10:5).

Guilt steals energy possibly more than any other thing simply because we are not designed by God to continually feel bad about ourselves. God loves us and wants us to keep our hearts light and free. Any thoughts that produce darkness should immediately be resisted in Jesus' name and replaced with ones that God approves of.

> *For the rest, brethren, whatever is true, whatever is worthy of reverence and is honorable and seemly, whatever is just, whatever is pure, whatever is lovely and lovable, whatever is kind and winsome and gracious, if there is any virtue and excellence,*

if there is anything worthy of praise, think on and weigh and take account of these things [fix your minds on them].

Philippians 4:8

Set Your Mind and Keep It Set

And set your minds and keep them set on what is above (the higher things), not on the things that are on the earth.

Colossians 3:2

To set our minds on what is above doesn't mean that we should sit around all day thinking about Heaven. It does mean that we should put our mind on God's will for us and the most excellent way to live. I love to say it this way: "Where the mind goes, the man follows." You can set your mind for the actions of the day with on-purpose thinking early in the morning. In other words, you can think about what you want to think about throughout the day. Perhaps it would go like this: *Today, I am going to think thoughts that will help me and other people. With the help of the Holy Spirit, I am going to think thoughts that will energize me and release joy in my life. I choose to think about what I can do for others, instead of thinking selfish thoughts. I have the mind of Christ* [see 1 Corinthians 2:16], *and I am going to use it to think like He would think.* This doesn't mean that all wrong thoughts will simply vanish, but it will make you more aware of them so you can cast them down and choose better ones (see 2 Corinthians 10:4–5).

I have learned that if I am tired, lacking energy, or even exhausted, thinking about it all day only makes it worse. When we feel bad, we usually think about it and talk about it so much that how we feel begins to consume us. When my husband doesn't feel good, he rarely talks about it. However, I tend to want people to know that I feel bad! I am sure that what I really want is some sympathy, but it doesn't make me feel better even if I do get it. I do know that thinking and talking about feeling bad or tired keeps me focused on it. If, on the other hand, I go do something and get my mind off of how I feel, I forget all about it. For women, shopping often helps us forget how bad we feel! It is amazing how much energy I can find if I run into a good sale. If you are a woman reading this, I am sure you know what I mean.

Energy is very important! It affects our creativity levels and ability to focus and has a huge impact on our desire and motivation to do things. It is sad how many people in the world are tired. It may be from lack of sleep, stress, poor food choices, and health problems, and each of those problems needs to be addressed, but a great deal of energy is lost through energy-draining thoughts! You can change yours into energy-producing thoughts, so I recommend that you start today!

Think About It!

- We won't become so tired of doing what we do in life if we are more careful concerning how we think about our lives.
- Don't wait for a feeling to motivate you. Choose your thoughts, stir yourself up, and do what God has placed in your heart to do.
- Fear robs your energy, but faith revives it.
- Negative thoughts—bitterness, guilt, discouragement, resentment, unforgiveness—always steal your energy.

SECTION 4

How Your Thoughts Affect Your Walk with God

CHAPTER 18

Thinking About What God Thinks About You

The worst loneliness is not to be comfortable with yourself.
Mark Twain

There are many voices that try to shape the way we think about every part of ourselves—our appearance, our abilities, our potential, and our identity. But those voices can be misleading. The opinions of the world, the accusations of our adversary, and our own thoughts and feelings don't define us.

The Bible teaches that the true identity, worth, and value of a believer is found in Christ. Our confidence is in Him (see Philippians 3:3). It doesn't matter what people think or say, or what our circumstances look like; we are defined by the fact that God loves and accepts us completely. To walk with God, we need to be in agreement with Him, and that involves learning to think as He thinks.

Wrong thinking about ourselves can lead to what I refer to as a case of "mistaken identity." I saw a movie about a woman who was sent to prison for something she didn't do because of a case of mistaken identity. Someone identified her as the guilty party, but they were wrong. When we have a case of mistaken identity, or we fail to know our worth and value as a child of God, we can also end up in prison. It may be an emotional prison of fear, self-hatred, poor self-image, lack of confidence, and many other unpleasant things. Jesus came to announce the release of the captives and the opening of the prison to those who are bound (see Isaiah 61:1).

He has opened the prison doors, but we must be willing to walk out of them and learn a new way of thinking and living. We can learn how to think about ourselves the way God thinks about us!

Today in our society we hear a lot about the dangers of having your identity stolen. People have even gone to the extreme of taking out insurance policies that cover them from such fraud and theft. I have wondered if what is happening in the world is a mirror image of what is happening to people in the spiritual realm. It seems that more and more in our society today people think their identity is found in success in business, financial status, social status, the neighborhood one lives in, level of education, et cetera. They are wrong. They are seeking an identity that can come crashing down at any moment. Henri Nouwen said it this way:

> Jesus came to announce to us that an identity based on success, popularity and power is a false identity—an illusion! Loudly and clearly He says: "You are not what the world makes you; but you are children of God."[1]

Jesus is our insurance policy against identity theft. When we know who we are in Him, then our value is secured for all time and cannot be shaken by anything. You are not loved because you are valuable—you are valuable because you are loved. Perhaps you have learned to be your own worst enemy, but now it is time to be your own best friend.

> You are not loved because you are valuable—you are valuable because you are loved.

Sally Field said, "It took me a long time not to judge myself through someone else's eyes."[2] We can know within ourselves who we are as children of God, and when we do, nothing can ever make us feel worthless and devalued. Meditate on this today: *God loves you!* If you think about that long enough, you will start to believe it, and when that happens you will begin to know how truly powerful you are.

Most of us enter our teenage years and young adulthood trying to prove through our accomplishments that we have value or that we are important. But the truth is that we are already important to God even before we accomplish anything in life. As a matter of fact, knowing that we are important to Him is what releases us to do great things for His glory, instead of our own.

This scripture gives us insight into this truth:

> Before I formed you in the womb I knew and approved of you [as My chosen instrument], and before you were born I separated and set you apart, consecrating you.
>
> Jeremiah 1:5

Reading a Scripture like this is helpful, but meditating on it (thinking about it over and over) is the most helpful. It renews our mind and teaches us to think in new ways that line up with God's will.

What Do You Think About You?

Have you ever taken any time to consider what you think about yourself? Most people have not, but it is an important thing to do. I can remember desperately struggling for most of my life with myself, but I finally learned to see myself as God does, and it revolutionized my life. My father had told me I was no good and would never amount to anything, but God tells me that I am His and that through Him, I can do greater things than I could ever imagine. It really isn't what other people think about us that hurts us, but it is what we think of ourselves!

God by His grace changes us on the inside, and then the Holy Spirit works with us, teaching us to live inside out! We are made right with God through faith in Christ. We are sanctified, and that means we are set apart and made holy by Him. These and many other wonderful works are accomplished in our spirits by God's grace. It is His gift to us! When we learn to believe what God has done in us, we will produce the fruit of it in our daily lives.

We may not do everything right, but God views us as right through our faith in Jesus and His work on the cross for us. The world places labels and assigns varying values to almost everything, but to God we are all equal. He loves and values each of us equally. We are all one in Christ!

I am not a mistake just because I make mistakes! Start meditating on that and speaking it out loud several times a day, and you will be a happier person. Don't spend your time thinking over and over about your faults. Don't compare yourself with other people, thinking that you should strive to be like them. Oscar Wilde said, "Be yourself; everyone else is already taken."[3]

> I am not a mistake just because I make mistakes!

Do you like yourself? I pray that you do, because you are going to spend every moment of your life with you. You will never get away from yourself, not even for a second, so I strongly suggest that you make peace with yourself if you haven't already done so, and learn to think about yourself the way God does.

None of us will ever go beyond what we think of ourselves. If we think we cannot do something, then we won't be able to do it.

Theodore Roosevelt said, "Believe you can and you're already half-way there."[4] More importantly, Jesus said in Matthew 21:22 (NIV), "If you believe, you will receive whatever you ask for in prayer."

Do you believe that you can do whatever you need to do in life through Christ Who is your strength (see Philippians 4:13)? Most people have a great deal more ability than is ever released in their life because they doubt their abilities. They assume they can't, without ever finding out if they can!

A very popular children's story is not only helpful to children, but can also be helpful to us as adults. It is called "The Story of the Engine That Thought It Could."

In a certain railroad yard there stood an extremely heavy train that had to be drawn up an unusually heavy grade before it could reach its destination. The superintendent of the yard was not sure what was best for him to do, so he went up to a large, strong engine and asked: "Can you pull that train over the hill?"

"It is a very heavy train," responded the engine.

He then went to another great engine and asked: "Can you pull that train over the hill?"

"It is a very heavy grade," it replied.

The superintendent was much puzzled, but he turned to still another engine that was spick and span new, and he asked it: "Can you pull that train over the hill?"

"I think I can," responded the engine.

So the order was circulated, and the engine was started back so that it might be coupled with the train, and as it went along the rails it kept repeating to itself: "I think I can. I think I can. I think I can."

The coupling was made and the engine began its journey, and all along the level, as it rolled toward the ascent,

it kept repeating to itself: "I...think...I can. I...think...
I...can. I...think...I...can."

Then it reached the grade, but its voice could still be
heard: "I think I can. I...think...I...can. I...think...
I...can." Higher and higher it climbed, and its voice grew
fainter and its words came slower: "I...think...I...can."

It was almost to the top.

"I...think."

It was at the top.

"I...can."

It passed over the top of the hill and began crawling
down the opposite slope.

"I...think...I...can...I...thought...I...could...I...
thought...I...could. I thought I could. I thought I could.
I thought I could."

And singing its triumph, it rushed on down toward
the valley.

Go through life saying, "I think I can," and you will be
amazed at what you will accomplish. When we have confidence,
it empowers us to be all we can be. Positive thinking that is in
agreement with God's Word releases the power and ability of God
in us. How often do you say, "I don't think I can," but you haven't
even tried yet? Keep your eyes on Jesus, not on yourself, and you
will be surprised at what you can do with His help.

Are You an Eagle Who Thinks It Is a Chicken?

While walking through the forest one day, a man found a
young eagle who had fallen out of his nest. He took it home
and put it in his barnyard where it soon learned to eat and
behave like the chickens. One day a naturalist passed by the

farm and asked why it was that the king of all birds should be confined to live in the barnyard with the chickens. The farmer replied that since he had given it chicken feed and trained it to be a chicken, it had never learned to fly. Since it now behaved as the chickens, it was no longer an eagle.

"Still it has the heart of an eagle," replied the naturalist, "and can surely be taught to fly." He lifted the eagle toward the sky and said, "You belong to the sky and not to the earth. Stretch forth your wings and fly." The eagle, however, was confused. He did not know who he was, and seeing the chickens eating their food, he jumped down to be with them again.

The naturalist took the bird to the roof of the house and urged him again, saying, "You are an eagle. Stretch forth your wings and fly." But again the eagle was afraid of his unknown self and the world and jumped down once more for the chicken food.

Finally the naturalist took the eagle out of the barnyard to a high mountain. There he held the king of the birds high above him and encouraged him again, saying, "You are an eagle. You belong to the sky. Stretch forth your wings and fly." The eagle looked around, back towards the barnyard and up to the sky. Then the naturalist lifted him straight towards the sun and it happened that the eagle began to tremble. Slowly he stretched his wings, and with a triumphant cry, soared away into the heavens.

It may be that the eagle still remembers the chickens with nostalgia. It may even be that he occasionally revisits the barnyard. But as far as anyone knows, he has never returned to lead the life of a chicken.[5]

We can see from this story that no matter how strongly the naturalist believed the eagle was an eagle, he continued to behave as a chicken until his own thinking and belief about himself changed. God already believes in you; now you can learn to think differently about yourself. Are you an eagle that has believed the lie that you are a chicken? If so, it is time to get out of the chicken yard and learn to fly!

What Does God Think About You?

Perhaps it never even occurred to you that God thinks about you, but He does.

> *Many, O Lord my God, are the wonderful works which You have done, and Your thoughts toward us; no one can compare with You! If I should declare and speak of them, they are too many to be numbered.*
>
> Psalm 40:5

God's thoughts toward us are found in His Word. His Word reveals His will. His Word is His thoughts written down for us to see. Psalm 139 is a beautiful psalm by David that teaches us a great deal about how God views us.

> *How precious and weighty also are Your thoughts to me, O God! How vast is the sum of them!*
> *If I could count them, they would be more in number than the sand.*
>
> Psalm 139:17–18

David declares that God's thoughts toward him (and us) are so many that they are like grains of sand on the beach. They are far too many to count and they are precious! God never thinks bad things about you! How awesome is that? It is highly probable that everyone we know occasionally thinks bad things about us, even if they truly love us. But God *never* thinks even one bad thought toward us!

I think that God has His mind on us all the time. Because He is God, He can think about each of us individually at one time, all the time, and yet it is still very personal.

God has His mind on us all the time.

I am sure He thinks about our possibilities more than our problems. I feel that He thinks about how far we have come, and not how far we have to go. David spoke of how God had created him and then declared that God's works are all wonderful! God must think that you are wonderful! Don't blush—just receive the good news! Yes, God thinks you are wonderful. Isn't that great to get into your heart?

In the story of creation, after each day of creating, God looked over His work and said, "It is good!"

Actually, He said, "It is very good." (See Genesis 1:31.)

In Isaiah 55:8–9, we learn that God's thoughts are higher than our thoughts. He thinks better things than we do; therefore, we should learn to think like He does. God not only has thoughts toward us, but He also has a plan.

> *For I know the thoughts and plans that I have for you, says the Lord, thoughts and plans for welfare and peace and not for evil, to give you hope in your final outcome.*
>
> Jeremiah 29:11

I find it quite amazing that God, Who I assume is busy running the universe, has time to think about me at all, let alone have a good plan for my life, but He does. It is because you and I are important to Him. Since you are here, God can use you—you have a purpose. There are things that you can do that nobody else can do exactly the way you can. He loves to hear your voice and when He looks at you, He smiles!

As you learn to think like God thinks, it will greatly improve your walk with Him and help you become more and more like Him. As you learn to think about yourself the way God thinks about you, it will change every area of your life. As a matter of fact, how you think about yourself may be one of the most important things you need to examine. Line your thinking up with God's thinking, and you are well on your way to an amazing life, walking with God each step of the way.

Think About It!

- The Word of God is what defines you, not the opinions of the world, the accusations of your adversary, or your own thoughts and feelings.
- You are important to God, even before you accomplish a single thing in life.
- It's not what other people think about you that helps or hurts you; it's what you choose to think about yourself.
- When you learn to believe what God has done for you, it will produce daily fruit in your life.
- Keep your eyes on Jesus, not on yourself, and you will be surprised at what you can do with His help.

CHAPTER 19

Thoughts and Behavior

Thoughts are boomerangs returning to their source. Choose wisely which ones you throw.

Unknown

Did you ever think of thoughts as something you throw out into the atmosphere, waiting to see what they bring back? It is a new idea for me, but an interesting one. God's Word backs it up when it says, "For as he thinks in his heart, so is he" (Proverbs 23:7). We all know what a boomerang is. You can throw it in any direction and it comes back to you. Thoughts are like that. I can throw out one that says, *I am no good and I will never accomplish anything valuable in life*, and that is exactly what comes back to me. We behave according to what we believe about ourselves.

When it comes to Christian behavior, I think that any serious-minded Christian truly wants to behave the way God urges him to in the Bible. We are taught to be loving, kind, good, humble, gentle, generous, patient, and self-controlled. We are taught to bear good fruit in every area of life. Our behavior should preach our sermons for us, and we should use words only when absolutely necessary. As a matter of fact, words without behavior to back it up can do a lot more harm than good. A hypocrite is someone who tells other people what to do but does not do it himself. Jesus had many heated conversations with religious people whom He referred to as hypocritical.

> *I therefore, the prisoner for the Lord, appeal to and beg you to walk (lead a life) worthy of the [divine] calling to which you have been called [with behavior that is a credit to the summons to God's service].*
>
> Ephesians 4:1

God's Word says that we are to live as Christ lived, love as He loved, think with His mind, and feel what He feels. It sounds like a daunting task, and we often turn the task into a nightmare of frustration and failed effort simply because we try to be good while at the same time we have bad thoughts.

> *Behold my affliction and my pain and forgive all my sins [of thinking and doing].*
>
> Psalm 25:18

This Scripture makes it clear that sinful thinking precedes sinful behavior. We cannot change our behavior unless we are willing to first be accountable for the thoughts that we meditate on.

Sinful thinking precedes sinful behavior.

A walk consists of many steps. As we walk with God, these steps are decisions that we make along the way about many things. We should use our free will to choose God's will. When we make right choices, God's grace is always available to help us follow through.

Ways to Renew the Mind

God offers us a new life, but His Word makes it clear that we must completely renew our mind (learn to think differently) before we will experience the new life He offers. We need to learn to think as God thinks, and that means we think according to God's Word. We are not to be conformed to the world and its ways of thinking and doing, but we are transformed (changed entirely) by the renewal of our mind (see Romans 12:2). This renewal doesn't take place automatically, but it is something we need to choose to do. It is a process and requires a commitment of time and effort.

There are multitudes of people who believe in Jesus, but they never experience victory in their lives due to a lack of knowledge or an unwillingness to apply the principles they have learned. I spent many years as a Christian who attended church regularly before ever discovering that my mind had anything to do with my behavior. I lacked knowledge. Then after acquiring the knowledge, I still had to be willing to go through the process, and I am still going through it even to this day. We will never have a day in our lives when we don't have to choose to cast down wrong thoughts and replace them with good ones.

The good news is that although it is quite a battle in the beginning, it does get easier as time goes by. We learn to recognize wrong and destructive thinking much quicker, and because we have learned the value of thinking properly, we can immediately choose thoughts that benefit us and help us enjoy God's plan for our lives.

Declaring God's Word is one of the most effective ways to renew your mind. As we speak it out loud, it begins to change us. We are learning to think differently. We also establish what we are choosing to believe in the unseen or spiritual realm, and it releases angels to help us and work on our behalf.

Bless (affectionately, gratefully praise) the Lord, you His angels, you mighty ones who do His commandments, hearkening to the voice of His word.

Psalm 103:20

As I mentioned previously, renewing your mind in order to understand your identity as a child of God is important. We cannot behave in a way that we don't believe is possible for us. If I think it is impossible for me to ever behave the way Jesus did, then I will never do so. When we receive Christ, God plants the seeds of godly behavior in us, and as we water them with the Word and spend time with God, those seeds grow and produce the fruit of godly behavior. Once we have a new image of ourselves and of our capabilities, our behavior changes without us struggling. We will need to make an effort, but it is an effort in and with the grace of God, not a struggle that produces frustration and failure.

I am going to include here a list of things for you to think and confess out loud about yourself. This has been compiled from God's Word and is therefore true. Go ahead and read it aloud!

I am greatly loved by God.

Romans 1:7; Ephesians 2:4; Colossians 3:12;
1 Thessalonians 1:4

I am strong in the Lord and the power of His might.

Colossians 1:11

I do not have a spirit of fear, but of power, love, and a sound mind.

2 Timothy 1:7

I let go of what lies behind and press toward the things ahead.

Philippians 3:12–14

I have favor with God.

2 Corinthians 13:14

I am complete in Him Who is the Head of all powers.

Colossians 2:10

I am alive with Christ.

Ephesians 2:5

I am free from the law of sin and death.

Romans 8:2

I am far from oppression, and fear does not come near me.

Isaiah 54:14

I am born of God, and the evil one does not touch me.

1 John 5:18

I am holy and without blame before Him in love.

Ephesians 1:4; 1 Peter 1:16

I have the mind of Christ.

1 Corinthians 2:16; Philippians 4:7

I have the peace that passes all understanding.

Philippians 4:7

I have the Greater One living in me; greater is He Who is in me than he who is in the world.

1 John 4:4

I have received the gift of righteousness and reign as a king in life by Jesus Christ.

Romans 5:17

I have received the spirit of wisdom and revelation in the knowledge of Jesus, the eyes of my understanding being enlightened.

Ephesians 1:17–18

I have God's power available to me as believer in Jesus.

Ephesians 1:19

I have received the power of the Holy Spirit to lay hands on the sick and see them recover, to cast out demons, to speak with new tongues. I have power and authority over all the power of the enemy, and nothing shall by any means harm me.

Mark 16:17–18; Luke 10:17–19

I have put off the old man and have put on the new man, which is renewed in knowledge after the image of Him Who created me.

Colossians 3:9–10

I give and it is given unto me; good measure, pressed down, shaken together, and running over, men give into my bosom.

Luke 6:38

I have no lack, for my God supplies all of my needs according to His riches in glory by Christ Jesus.

Philippians 4:19

I can quench all the fiery darts of the wicked one as I lift up my shield of faith.

Ephesians 6:16

I can do all things through Christ Jesus.

Philippians 4:13

God has called me out of darkness into His marvelous light.

1 Peter 2:9

I am God's child, for I am born again of the incorruptible seed of the Word of God, which lives and abides forever.

1 Peter 1:23

I am God's workmanship, created in Christ to do good works.

Ephesians 2:10

I am a new creature in Christ; old things have passed away.

2 Corinthians 5:17

I am a doer of the Word and blessed in my actions.

James 1:22, 25

I am a joint heir with Christ.

Romans 8:17

I am more than a conqueror through Him Who loves me.

Romans 8:37

I am an overcomer by the blood of the Lamb and the word of my testimony.

Revelation 12:11

I am a partaker of God's divine nature.

2 Peter 1:3–4

I am an ambassador for Christ (I represent Him).

2 Corinthians 5:20

I am part of a chosen generation, a royal priesthood, a holy nation, a purchased people.

1 Peter 2:9

I am the righteousness of God in Christ.

2 Corinthians 5:21

I am the temple of the Holy Spirit: I am not my own.

1 Corinthians 6:19

I am the head and not the tail; I am above only and not beneath.

Deuteronomy 28:13

It is God's will that I prosper and have good health.

3 John 1:2

I delight myself in God's Word and all that I do prospers and succeeds.

Psalm 1:2–3

Jesus understands me, and even when I make mistakes, I can pray boldly and He helps me.

Hebrews 4:15–16

When I am weary I run to Jesus and He refreshes me.

Matthew 11:28

I am healed by the stripes of Jesus.

Isaiah 53:5; 1 Peter 2:24

I meditate on the Word of God and I do what is written in it,
and I prosper in my way, deal wisely, and have good success.

Joshua 1:8

The more your mind is renewed by these things that God says about you in His Word, the more your behavior will improve.

Now, if you want to get an even greater benefit from the confessions I have just suggested, you can use them daily, and when possible take the time to look up each Scripture; read them and think about them for a few minutes. The Word of God has power in it to save our souls when we approach it with meekness (see James 1:21). You cannot change yourself, or force yourself to behave better, but you can ask God to help you, and He will use His Word to grant you the strength and discipline that you need. God changes us from one degree of glory to another as we study His Word (see 2 Corinthians 3:18). We have already seen that with God's help we can choose to walk as Jesus walked (behave as He did). God's Word transforms us into the image of Jesus, and our behavior changes for the better.

We renew our minds by studying, reading, and hearing God's Word. We also renew our minds when we declare it out loud. The more we meditate on the Word of God, the more our minds are renewed (changed, transformed).

Taking Thoughts Captive

The renewal of the mind also requires us to be willing to think about what we think about and to take wrong thoughts captive to the obedience of Christ. Thoughts that will need to be taken captive are ones that come from the devil or the mind of the flesh. God's Word teaches us that we have a mind of the flesh that produces death and all kinds of misery and a mind of the Spirit that produces life (see Romans 8:6). If we live according to the flesh, it is because we are thinking with the mind of the flesh, and if we live according to the Spirit, it is because we are thinking with the mind of the Spirit. Thoughts precede behavior!

> *For those who are according to the flesh and are controlled by its unholy desires set their minds on and pursue those things which gratify the flesh, but those who are according to the Spirit and are controlled by the desires of the Spirit set their minds on and seek those things which gratify the [Holy] Spirit.*
>
> Romans 8:5

If I want to walk in love, I cannot spend excessive time thinking about myself and what I want and need. I will need to think about things I can do to help others and show them love. If I want to be unselfish and free from self-centeredness, I cannot have my mind on myself all the time. If I want to lose some weight, I can't think about food all the time. If I feel an urgency to eat, but know that I really don't need to eat yet, I should do something and get my mind off of food and the "I have to eat" feeling will go away.

If I want to get out of debt, I should not spend an hour a day reading all the sale catalogs and advertisements that come in the mail, because they will fill my mind with things I want, things that I probably don't need at all.

If I want to get my house cleaned up, then I should not think about how tedious the cleaning will be. Put your thoughts into what you (the spiritual you) truly want to do, not just merely what your flesh is demanding at the moment. If you or I want to change anything about our behavior, we must first change our thinking about that behavior. When we think about something, we make provision for it. Consider this word of advice from God through the apostle Paul.

> *But clothe yourself with the Lord Jesus Christ (the Messiah), and make no provision for [indulging] the flesh [put a stop to thinking about the evil cravings of your physical nature] to [gratify its] desires (lusts).*
>
> Romans 13:14

Please take time to go over this Scripture several times. It completely backs up the message of this book. We make provision for wrong behavior by thinking about it! Our excuse for wrong thinking has always been to believe that we just cannot help what we think, but that is not true. When I finally saw that I could choose my own thoughts with God's help, it was the beginning of an amazing life change. You can do your own thinking! Martin Luther King said it this way:

> As long as the mind is enslaved, the body can never be free.[1]

I admit that it is a battle at first, just as anything is that we have never done before, but soon you will form new habits and be well on your way to manifesting the godly behavior that you desire.

Think About It!

- We behave according to what we believe about ourselves.
- When you make right choices, God's grace is always available to help you follow through.
- It is essential to renew your mind in order to experience the new life God offers.
- The more you do it, the easier it is to recognize wrong and destructive behavior.
- When you have a right image of yourself, your behavior changes without struggle.
- The more you meditate on the Word of God, the more your mind is renewed.

CHAPTER 20

The Mind-Mouth Connection

Be careful of your thoughts; they may become words at any moment.

Ira Gassen

The connection between what we think and what we say is stronger than most people realize. We will never change what we say if we don't understand how important what we say is! Words are not empty or harmless. Words are containers filled with power, and we choose whether that power will be negative or positive. We can bless or curse with the words of our mouth. We can build up or tear down. We can make people laugh or make them cry. God wants to use us to advance His Kingdom. He wants us to partner with Him in introducing people to Him, and just as we can learn to think as God does, we can also learn to talk as He talks.

Mother Teresa said, "Words which do not give the light of Christ increase the darkness."[1] It is important that we choose words that are pleasing to Christ, and if they are, they will generally please everyone. According to the book of Proverbs, we must be satisfied with the consequences of our words. Words have consequences!

Death and life are in the power of the tongue.

Proverbs 18:21

The apostle James had a lot to say about the power of words. In James 3, he says that although the tongue is a little member, it can boast of great things. The tiny spark of a word can start a large fire. He says that the tongue is a world of wickedness and a wild animal that no man can tame. Wow!

James compares the power of the tongue to the power that a small rudder has to turn around a huge ship, or how a tiny bit in the horse's mouth is used to turn its whole body about. James is saying that the things we speak out of our mouths can determine the direction of our lives. Oh my! If we believe that, we should make some quick changes. I won't go so far as to say that everything we speak is what we end up with, but I do strongly believe that words have amazing power, and if we persist in speaking ungodly and negative things, it will definitely harm and hinder the plan of God for us.

It was many years before I had any idea that my own thoughts and words had tremendous influence on my life and behavior. For example, due to being abused and controlled by my father, I repeatedly said to myself, as well as to others, "When I get out of this house, nobody is ever going to tell me what to do again." I became very rebellious toward authority, and especially male authority. When Dave and I got married, I learned in God's Word that God wanted me to respect and admire Dave's opinions and to honor him as the head of our home, but I was totally unable to do so. I wanted to, but I could not!

It took some time and some strong lessons from the Holy Spirit before I learned that I had imprisoned myself in rebellion by the words I said for years when I was younger. I had actually made a vow to myself that I would not let anyone ever tell me what to do. I finally saw my error and repented, asking God to forgive me and to soften my hardened heart toward authority. It took some time, but as I grew in God and changed my thinking and speaking, my mind was renewed and I was set free.

You may remember earlier when I mentioned that I smoked cigarettes. I was addicted; I smoked for about twenty years, and I repeatedly said, "I know I could never quit smoking, because if I did I would gain weight. It would just be too hard to quit." Years later when I did desire to quit, I found myself in a greater struggle than I could handle on my own. Dave decided to quit and did, but I could not seem to break free. As I prayed about the habit and asked God to help me, He led me to start saying out loud that I was quitting smoking—that it was a bad habit, costly, smelly, and not good for my health. Amazingly, within a few weeks I had no desire to smoke again. I'm happy to say that was forty years ago.

Words definitely have power. Many people with addictions say over and over that the addiction is too strong for them to break it or that they will never be free from it, and sure enough they end up being right. It would be most helpful for anyone trying to overcome an addiction or break any bad habit to begin confessing what they want to see happen, instead of confessing that they will never be free.

Would God approve of such behavior? Surprisingly, the Bible states that God does the same thing. God had promised Abraham that he would become the father of many nations, but for a long time, Abraham had no children. God changed his name from Abram, meaning "high, exalted father," to Abraham, which meant "father of a multitude" (see Genesis 17:5). Names and their meanings carried much more weight in Abraham's day than they do today. Therefore, each time God or anyone else called Abraham's name, they were declaring that Abraham would indeed father a multitude.

We read in the book of Romans that God gives life to the dead, and calls things that are not in existence as if they are (see Romans 4:17). God speaks things into existence. He used words to create the world, and it is with His Word that He currently upholds and maintains the universe (see Hebrews 1:3). Perhaps you have no difficulty believing that God's words have power, but you doubt that your own do. Perhaps it will help if you remember that you are created in God's image and told to imitate Him.

> *So God created man in His own image, in the image and likeness of God He created him; male and female He created them.*
>
> Genesis 1:27

> *Therefore be imitators of God [copy Him and follow His example], as well-beloved children [imitate their father].*
>
> Ephesians 5:1

Think Before You Speak

I am sure somebody has said to you at some time in your life, "Think before you speak." The truth is that much of what we think literally falls out of our mouths with no forethought as to how it is going to sound or what it may create. We can learn to discipline ourselves enough not to say everything that floats through our mind, but if we meditate on something frequently we will usually end up saying it. Even if it is something we would not want anyone to know we were thinking—in an unguarded moment, we blurt it out.

I was with a friend recently who was wearing something that did not compliment her body shape. The more I thought how bad I thought it looked on her, the more difficult it became for me not to tell her. Sadly, I did end up telling her (in love, of course!), but I realized immediately that my comment made her feel bad. I even went about trying to fix my blunder by saying, "What you're wearing just doesn't do you justice; you would look better if the top was shorter, blah, blah, blah!" I finally just simply said, "I am so sorry I said that." She said, "I knew it didn't look the best on me, but it was new and I just wanted to wear it." The moment I had the thought about her clothing choice, I should have whispered to myself, "Joyce, it is none of your business what she wears." Thankfully, we are really good friends and she didn't get angry, but God let me know that I had been really foolish.

This is one tiny example of how I can blurt things out without thinking about the damage it will do, and perhaps you have this *wonderful* ability also. I thought something, I spoke it, it hurt my friend, and it all happened in a few moments. It is frightening how quickly things can go through our minds and fall out of our mouths.

I think it is nearly impossible for us to control our mouths unless we first learn to control our minds. We cannot do either without the grace (help) of God, so the first thing to do is pray. The Psalmist David prayed regularly that the meditations of his heart and the words of his mouth would be acceptable to God (see Psalm 19:14). He also prayed that God would set a guard over his mouth and keep watch at the door of his lips (see Psalm 141:3). David knew that he needed God's help in this very important area. Both of these Scriptures are good ones to pray daily.

A Word Is a Thought Revealed

When we speak, our thought life is being turned inside out. If we don't want our thoughts to be revealed, then we better not think them too long, because if we do, they usually find a way to get out. Jesus said that what is in the heart comes out of the mouth (see Matthew 12:34), and Jesus is always right. It is not safe to keep thinking something

> When we speak, our thought life is being turned inside out.

if you really don't want to end up saying it. Of course, there is a chance you might control yourself and never say what you think, but I believe it is better not to take the chance. I think the connection between the mind and the mouth may be the strongest one we experience. When the two join together and are in agreement, the rest of our fate is sealed. If I think angry thoughts and speak angry words, I will begin to feel angry in my emotions, and more than likely I will display angry behavior toward someone before too long. The mind connection is powerful indeed!

We may not always tell a person if we are thinking something bad about them. But we usually do end up telling someone, and that someone may tell someone, and so on and so forth, until we have created a huge problem that could have been avoided if we had only chosen to think something good. We can overcome evil only with good—nothing else works (see Romans 12:21).

In learning how to cast down wrong thoughts and imaginations, I learned that the only way to eliminate the bad ones and keep them from returning was to fill my mind with something good. That way when the bad ones returned (and they always do), they found no place to enter.

Take No Thought, Saying…

The apostle Matthew teaches us not to worry and speak the worry out of our mouth: "Do not worry, saying, 'What shall we eat?' or 'What shall we drink?' or 'What shall we wear?'" (Matthew 6:31 NIV). I have a lot of experience with worry, and perhaps you do also. It seems to be something that is fairly easy for most of us to do. It is interesting how much time we put into worrying, but it is totally useless. As soon as a problem occurs, the natural impulse is to worry, but we can quickly trade it in for trusting God. Trust is God's antidote for worry and anxiety. When I find myself worrying, I often say out loud, "God, I trust You." I discovered long ago that the way to break a thought pattern that I don't want is to say something else. It gives us enough time to take back control of our thoughts and redirect them. It is true that what is in our heart comes out of our mouth, but it is also true that what we speak out of our mouths will get into our hearts. We can renew our thinking with purposeful words.

God has given us the gift and the responsibility of thoughts and words, so let us use them wisely. Let's put them to work in our lives in a way that will be pleasing to Him.

If you have never paid much attention to disciplining your thoughts, this may seem like a mountain that you are not sure you can tackle, but if I can do it, anybody can. I had huge problems in this area. Not little ones, *huge* ones. Little by little with God's help and persistence, I have experienced major changes in how my mind functions.

It seems like a fairly easy task now to simply not think something that I know isn't a good thing. Of course, I am not always successful, but I succeed more than I fail now, and that is progress worth celebrating. I frequently study in this area, because it is quite easy to fall back into bad habits and start fires with my tongue that I cannot put out. Take God's Word like you would take medicine. If you are weak in any area, then study in that area and you will begin to improve. Study thoughts, the mind, words, the mouth, and the tongue. You will be amazed at how many Scripture verses God has included in the Bible on these subjects. There are too many to ignore or to take lightly.

I teach and write frequently on this subject, because there is no hope of anyone enjoying the life that Jesus died to give us without having insight into these areas. The apostle Peter said that if we want to enjoy life, we must keep our tongues free from evil and our lips from guile (see 1 Peter 3:10).

The apostle James said that if anyone thinks himself to be religious and does not bridle his tongue, then his religious service is useless (see James 1:26). To bridle your tongue means to control it. God has given us the fruit of self-control that we might be able to allow or disallow behaviors in our own lives. We can learn what behaviors benefit us and God's Kingdom and which behaviors do not, and thankfully we can choose accordingly.

I can say with great conviction that in these areas God has taught me some of the most life-changing lessons I've ever learned, and I believe it will have the same effect on you. If you need to, read this chapter again and again until you feel it has become part of you. With God's help, learn to control your thoughts and not let your mind run wild. Don't let the devil use it as a garbage dump. Choose your thoughts carefully, keeping in mind they will become your words and ultimately your feelings and behavior.

> Listen (consent and submit) to the words of the wise, and apply your mind to my knowledge;
> For it will be pleasant if you keep them in your mind [believing them]; your lips will be accustomed to [confessing] them.
>
> Proverbs 22:17–18

This Scripture teaches us that if we keep God's Word in our mind, it will be pleasant. Life will turn out better for us. Not only will we think on God's Word, but also our lips will be accustomed to confessing it. What we allow ourselves to meditate on and to declare influences our destiny!

How we view the power of words will determine how we use

them. Here are some things I suggest that you ponder concerning how to think about your words:

- Words have great influence.
- They reveal what is in your mind.
- Words can hurt or heal.
- Words can cause someone to keep going or to give up.
- Words contain the power of life and death.
- We have to eat our words and deal with their consequences.
- God hears all of our words.
- Right words can put smiles on people's faces.
- Words can bring comfort.
- Words spoken in anger are unwise.
- Keep your word to God and to other people.

The more we realize the power and influence that words have, the more careful we will be with them.

Think About It!

- Words are not merely words. They are containers filled with power.
- If you speak and think negative things, it will harm and hinder God's plan for your life.
- If you are trying to break a habit, confess what you want to see instead of what you can never be.
- Prayer is always the first step in controlling what thoughts you think and what words you say.
- Trust is God's antidote for worry and anxiety.
- What you allow yourself to meditate on and to declare influences your destiny.

CHAPTER 21

How to Get Your Mind Back When You Feel Like You Have Lost It!

I will be calm; I will be mistress of myself.

Jane Austen, *Sense and Sensibility*

We frequently hear people say, "I feel like I am losing my mind!" What do they mean? They are usually worried, anxious, fearful, and feeling overwhelmed by having too much to do in life. We have all felt that way at times and more than likely we have made that statement.

When we feel as if we are losing our mind, it is due to not controlling the thoughts we allow to go through it. When too many thoughts rush in and pile up on top of each other, and we can find no solution to any of the problems they represent, it is because we have not exercised self-control with our thoughts sooner.

I like Jane Austen's statement: "I *will* be calm; I *will* be mistress of myself."[1] Doing so is a decision that only strong determination helps us follow through on. God has given us all the peace we need to live without pressure in a world that is filled with pressure everywhere we turn. We do live in the world, but thankfully we don't have to live as the world lives. We can have the peace of God in the midst of the storms of life.

Before we can enjoy peace of mind, we must truly believe that we have self-control. We have the ability to control our thoughts, words, and actions! If we don't believe it, we will never do it. Should you ever feel that you are losing your mind, the first step to take in getting it back is to take a quick inventory of the thoughts racing through it and eliminate all the ones that are stealing your peace. You may be thinking, *Come on, Joyce. It is not that easy.* I didn't say it was easy, but I am saying that it is possible.

I can recall praying often, "Oh God, grant me peace of mind. I don't think I can take this much longer." I have had to learn in my life that I often pray wrong. I ask for things that God has already given me but that I am failing to access by faith. Please examine this Scripture carefully and ask yourself if you believe it or not.

> *Peace I leave with you; My [own] peace I now give and bequeath to you. Not as the world gives do I give to you. Do not let your hearts be troubled, neither let them be afraid. [Stop allowing yourselves to be agitated and disturbed; and do not permit yourselves to be fearful and intimidated and cowardly and unsettled.]*
>
> John 14:27

This Scripture clearly places the responsibility for receiving His peace on us. Jesus has already given us peace. You may say, "Well, if that is true, then where is it, and why don't I feel peaceful?" You cannot wait to feel it in order to believe you have it. We access all the promises of God by believing them. God calls us to walk by faith and not by sight or feelings (see 2 Corinthians 5:7). I frequently say that we are like people trying to get into a chair we are already sitting in. Just imagine the uselessness and frustration of such an effort. If you're in the chair, then just relax and enjoy it. Jesus left us His peace, and if you believe it, you will begin to enjoy it.

Peace from God is only one of countless promises that God has given us through Jesus. Think it over—are there other things you are begging God to give you that you already have? I am sure there are many, but self-control may be one of them. You have self-control, and it is waiting for you to exercise it. Self-control is a friend that God gives us to help us be the person we truly want to be and do the things we truly want to do. Some other things that we have in our spirit as gifts from God are love, joy, patience, humility, kindness, goodness, power, mercy, and ability. We start by believing we have them, and they are developed as we use them again and again with God's help.

The problems of life that come against us are opportunities to exercise the good things that God has filled us with. I will never develop patience if I never have a need to be patient. I will never develop mercy unless I need to give it to someone who really doesn't deserve it. I will never develop self-control unless I am tempted to lose control.

The Tipping Point

I think we all have a tipping point and we can learn to recognize what it feels like when we are reaching it. You may be able to do two or even three things at one time, balancing them in such a way that they all get done without causing you stress, but at what point are you overwhelmed? What if the two or three things become ten things? Is that too much, or can you still take more?

We are each created differently, perfectly adapted for the call on our lives. I had an amazing ability to multitask in my earlier years because of what God had called me to do. The ministry was in the early, foundation-laying years, and the workload involved was quite heavy. Back in those days, let's say theoretically that I could easily handle juggling four problems at a time and still stay calm. Today that is different. I am older and in a different season of my life. Two is about my maximum these days. If I go over that, I start to feel that I am reaching my tipping point.

I have trained myself to recognize when I am on the verge of losing my peace, and I pull back and eliminate one of the things causing the problem. After almost forty years of experience walking with God, I know how important it is for me to keep my peace! By the way, God's Word doesn't say, "When you're upset, go get some peace," but it does say to "hold your peace" (see Exodus 14:14).

If I don't take action to eliminate one or more of my stressors, I will get into that danger zone we are all familiar with. You know, the one where we feel like we are losing our mind, and then we lose control of our mouth and start saying all kinds of things we will be sorry for later, and then we start behaving in ways that embarrass us when we calm down and realize how we acted.

You may think that you have to deal with everything that is thrown at you, and you have no way of eliminating any of the things causing you to feel overwhelmed, but that simply is not true. God will never give us more to handle than we can handle calmly. If I am overloaded, it is my own fault. I have not managed my schedule well, I have said yes to too many things; I am trying to please all the people I know instead of being led by the Holy Spirit. Or I may be a workaholic who feels validated only when I am working and can complain to people about how much I have to do.

If we start the elimination process when we sense we are reaching our tipping point—the place where we are about to go over the edge, so to speak, and start behaving badly—then we will never have to say or think, "I feel like I am losing my mind."

Regaining Control That Has Been Lost

If we don't make the decision to calm down early enough, then we will lose control, but even then it is not too late to regain control that has been lost. At any time we realize we are out of control, we can regain control by making a decision to do so. Here are some steps that will hopefully help in the process:

- **Step 1**—Stop talking! When we feel overwhelmed, we usually start talking to anyone who will listen, and if nobody is around, we are prone to talking anyway just to hear the sound of our frustrations. We will never regain control unless we stop talking and regroup!

- **Step 2**—Be as realistic as you can about what is really happening. Have you let yourself become more upset than the situation really calls for? Is the problem you are facing really as bad as you are imagining it to be? Are you worrying about things that have not even happened yet and may never happen?

- **Step 3**—As you begin to calm down, ask yourself if any of the things you feel overloaded with can be put off until later or perhaps handed off to someone else to deal with. Could you get help if you ask for it? Are you really the only one who can handle the things pressuring you? Only a foolish person thinks they can keep doing the same thing and get a different result. So if you truly want change in your circumstances, you will have to be willing to make some changes yourself.

- **Step 4**—Think about what you are thinking about that is frustrating you and stop thinking about it. Cast your care on God and let Him show you what He can do. Keep saying, "God, I let this go. I trust You!" Say it until you feel yourself calming down.

- **Step 5**—We can manage our emotions and learn to live beyond our feelings. Being the master or mistress of yourself under God's leadership is entirely possible, but it will not happen as long as you let raw emotion rule. We cannot prevent feelings from coming, but we don't have to let them control us. We are totally capable of using self-control even in the midst of the wildest emotion. It may be painful to our soul, but it will be worth it in the end. Absolutely nobody respects him- or herself when they are out of control!

- **Step 6**—Resist the devil at his onset! The root source of all lack of peace is the devil. It is not people or even circumstances. It is the devil working through the people or the circumstance. The devil has set you up to get you upset, and the sooner you realize it and take action to resist him, the easier it will be.

If you have lost your mind, where is it? You really have not lost it—you have just temporarily given up control of it, but you can regain it quickly by applying these steps. Purpose to do each one in a prayerful attitude, because we have no success at anything without God's help. However, when you pray, resist asking God to give you something that He clearly has stated in His Word that you already have. Instead of asking for peace, thank God that you have peace and ask Him to help you walk in it.

Preventing Mental Overload

Along with the steps previously mentioned, here are some important ways you can prevent mental overload and live the joyful, peaceful life Jesus died to give you:

- **Stay Strong**—Staying strong is much easier than allowing ourselves to get weak and in trouble. One of the ways we stay strong is to spend regular, quality time with God. Spending time studying God's Word and talking with Him prepares us for whatever may be waiting for us in our circumstances.

  We are not strong enough for any success in ourselves, but we are strong in the Lord and in the power of His might (see Ephesians 6:10).

  If we have a strong immune system, we will avoid a lot of sickness, and likewise, if we have a strong spirit, it will sustain us in times of pressure (see Proverbs 18:14).

- **Know Yourself**—It is wise to know your capabilities and limitations. I know that at this stage of my life I cannot handle as much as I once could and remain peaceful, so I just don't try to do it. Know yourself, and be satisfied to be yourself without comparing yourself with anyone else. I have friends who can do much more than I can, but I am not required to try and do what they do. We are responsible only to do what God wants us to do. He never puts more on us than we can bear!

  Don't feel like a weakling if you need to say, "That is more than I can handle." It is a wise person, indeed, who knows himself well, and does not push himself to be someone he is not!

- **Examine Your Thoughts**—Are your own thoughts draining your energy? If so, change what you are thinking, and think happy thoughts. Most of what makes people feel they are on overload is a fear of some sort that manifests in worry, anxiety, and pressure. Meditate on this: God has not given me a spirit of fear but of power, love, and a sound mind (see 2 Timothy 1:7). God's Word does contain more power than your worry. You will sense yourself calming down as you focus on God's Word, which truly acts as medicine for the soul.

- **Talk Yourself into a Change**—Should you feel that you are losing your mind, tell yourself that it is a lie and that you have self-control and a sound mind. Remind yourself that God is with you and that you can do whatever you need to do in life through Him.

  Have you ever talked with a person who was upset, and you succeeded in calming them down through talking to them? You can do the same thing with yourself. We can talk ourselves into and out of being upset! When I am sensing a loss of peace or a wrong attitude in myself, I say, "I have to have a chat with myself," and I do. It always helps!

- **Don't Get Discouraged**—If victory doesn't come quickly, don't get discouraged and give up. Some problems that we have are strongholds that Satan has had for a long time. They are areas he has dominated through his lies and deceptions, and those strongholds must be torn down. It takes time and a willingness to keep doing the right thing until you get a right result, no matter how long it takes.

- **Don't Feel Guilty**—When you have trouble keeping your mind in the proper condition, don't feel guilty. Everybody has trouble with wrong thoughts, and sometimes the trouble can be severe. As believers in Christ we are all growing in spiritual maturity and we may not be where we need to be, but thank God we are not where we used to be!

Piling up guilty thoughts on top of other troublesome thoughts can really make us feel that we are losing our mind, so remember to live in the "guilt-free zone" with Jesus, who has already paid for all of your sins.

Keep a good confession as you walk with God. Don't say things like, "I feel like I am losing my mind," or "I am going to lose my mind," or "If this continues, I am going to lose my mind." You will not lose your mind, and even if you misplace it, God will help you get it back.

Think About It!

- Self-control is the key to a godly thought life.
- You live in this world, but you don't have to live as this world lives. You can choose to live differently.
- Take an inventory of your thoughts and eliminate the ones that are stealing your peace.
- When you feel like you have lost control, there's still time to get it back.
- Jesus has already provided His peace. All you have to do is receive it.

As usual, by the time we get to the end of any book, we have taken in a lot of information, and we probably don't remember all of it. With that thought in mind, I would like to reiterate what I feel is the main theme of this book and what I hope it does for you.

Your thoughts affect every area of your life, so that makes them extremely important. They especially affect the words we speak, the attitudes and moods that we display, our relationships, including our personal relationship with God, and our success or failure in things that we do.

I encourage you to believe what God believes, learn to think as He would think, say what He says, and make the decisions that He leads you to make. God, through Jesus, has provided an amazing life for us, one in which we can bear much good fruit for God and mankind.

I recommend that you daily ask God to help you with your thoughts and words, because they are more important than any of us might imagine. Right ones are filled with life, and wrong ones are filled with death and misery of every kind. As I close, let us remember the words of God: "…**I have set before you life and death, the blessings and curses; therefore choose life, that you and your descendants may live.**" (Deuteronomy 30:19)

NOTES

Chapter 1: The Life You've Always Wanted to Live

1 http://www.brainyquote.com/quotes/quotes/t/thomasaed149049.html.
2 Thomas Fuller, *Gnomologia* (London: T. and J. Allman, 1817); quoted at https://www.goodreads.com/quotes/52802-all-things-are-difficult-before -they-are-easy.
3 http://www.brainyquote.com/quotes/quotes/f/frankacla165910.html.
4 http://www.goodreads.com/quotes/666437-if-you-want-to-turn-your-life -around-try-thankfulness.
5 http://www.brainyquote.com/quotes/quotes/e/erichoffer105510.html.
6 http://thinkexist.com/quotation/god_gave_you_a_gift_of_seconds_today -have_you/227289.html.

Chapter 2: Mind, Mouth, Moods, and Attitudes

1 http://www.goodreads.com/quotes/812245-you-are-never-too-old-to-set -another-goal-or.

Chapter 3: How to Think When Life Gets Difficult

1 http://www.goodreads.com/quotes/178548-if-you-don-t-like-something -change-it-if-you-can-t.
2 http://www.brainyquote.com/quotes/quotes/c/charlessta451677.html.

Chapter 4: Choose Your Attitude

1 Tim Stan, "In Tragedy's Aftermath, They Chose Love," *Guideposts* (http:// www.guideposts.org/inspiration/angels-on-earth/earth-angels/in-tragedy's -aftermath-they-chose-love.
2 "Oskar Schindler: His List of Life," http://www.oskarschindler.com.
3 Originally published in *Guideposts*; quoted in "Focus," Sermon Illustra- tions, http//www.sermonillustrations.com/a-z/f/focus.htm.
4 "Duke University Study," SermonSearch, http://www.sermonsearch.com/ sermon-illustrations/4525/duke-university-study/.

5 Anonymous, from "Short Stories on Positive Attitude," Paradise4Women .com, http://paradise4women.com /short-stories-on-positive-attitude/.

Chapter 5: Anyone Can Be Happy

1 http://www.goodreads.com/quotes/396401-joy-does-not-simply-happen -to-us-we-have-to.
2 http://thinkexist.com/quotation/it_isn-t_what_you_have-or_who_you_are -or_where/204180.html.
3 http://www.goodreads.com/quotes/69-folks-are-usually-about-as-happy -as-they-make-their.
4 http://www.goodreads.com/quotes/110985-it-s-been-my-experience-that -you-can-nearly-always-enjoy.
5 http://www.kentcrockett.com/cgi-bin/illustrations/index.cgi?topic=Joy.
6 Kim Gaines Eckert, "The Psychology of Happiness," *Christianity Today*, September 2013, http://www.christianitytoday.com/women/2013/september/ psychology-of-happiness.html.
7 Caroline Leaf, "Controlling Your Toxic Thoughts," Dr. Leaf, http://drleaf .com/about/toxic-thoughts/.

Chapter 6: The Power of Focus

1 http://www.values.com/inspirational-quotes/4443-no-horse-gets-anywhere -until-he-is-harnessed.
2 Carol Dweck, "The Mindset of Athletes," Mindset, http://www.mindsetonline .com/howmindsetaffects/sports/index.html.

Chapter 7: Would You Want to Be Friends with You?

1 http://thinkexist.com/quotation/any_fool_can_criticize-condemn-and _complain-and/202966.html.

Chapter 9: Thoughtless Actions

1 http://www.brainyquote.com/quotes/quotes/m/marktwain106287.html.

Chapter 10: The Power of Perspective

1 "I Love Nice Thought Provoking Stories," Experience Project, http://www .experienceproject.com/stories/Love-Nice-Thought-Provoking-Stories/ 2848792.

Chapter 11: What Do You Think About That Person?

1 Alexa Stevenson, "Probing Question: Does Talking to Plants Help Them Grow?" *Penn State News*, August 25, 2008, http://news.psu.edu/story/141343/ 2008/08/25/research/probing-question-does-talking-plants-help-them-grow.

2 Stephen Brown, *Christianity Today*, April 5, 1993, p. 17.

3 http://www.sermoncentral.com/illustrations/sermon-illustration-fred
-parker-stories-64295.asp.

4 http://www.goodreads.com/quotes/2887-if-you-judge-people-you-have
-no-time-to-love.

5 http://www.goodreads.com/quotes/209465-things-are-not-always-what
-they-seem-the-first-appearance.

6 Our Daily Bread, July 20, 1992.

Chapter 14: Your Thoughts and Stress

1 Source unknown, quoted in "Worry," Sermon Illustrations, http://www
.sermonillustrations.com/a-z/w/worry.htm.

2 Source unknown, quoted in "Stress," Sermon Illustrations, http://www
.sermonillustrations.com/a-z/s/stress.htm.

Chapter 15: The Mind-Body Connection

1 Dr. Caroline Leaf, *Switch on Your Brain* (Grand Rapids, MI: Baker Books,
2013), pp. 33–38.

2 Ed and Deb Shapiro, "How Your Thoughts and Emotions Can Affect Your
Body," *Huffington Post*, November 29, 2011, http://www.huffingtonpost
.com/ed-and-deb-shapiro/mind-body-relationship_b_1115165.html?
view=print&comm_ref=false.

Chapter 16: The Mind-Performance Connection

1 William Shakespeare, *Henry V*, quoted at http://www.goodreads.com/
quotes/119936-all-things-are-ready-if-our-mind-be-so.

2 http://www.brainyquote.com/quotes/quotes/m/michaeljor104651.html.

3 http://www.mindseyesports.com/quotes/.

4 http://www.baberuth.com/quotes/.

5 http://www.brainyquote.com/quotes/quotes/j/jacknickla400460.html.

6 http://www.mindseyesports.com/quotes/.

Chapter 17: Where Did All My Energy Go?

1 Philip Chircop, "Enthusiasm," A-Mused, November 6, 2012, http://www
.philipchircop.com/post/35151648435/enthusiasm-reflect-on-this-short
-story-and-then.

Chapter 18: Thinking About What God Thinks About You

1 https://www.goodreads.com/quotes/521136-jesus-came-to-announce-to
-us-that-an-identity-based.

2 http://www.brainyquote.com/quotes/quotes/s/sallyfield104637.html.

3 http://www.goodreads.com/quotes/19884-be-yourself-everyone-else-is
-already-taken.

4 http://www.brainyquote.com/quotes/quotes/t/theodorero380703.html.

5 "The Eagle," *Theology News and Notes*, October 1976; quoted in *Multnomah Message*, Spring 1993, p. 1; available at https://bible.org/illustration/eagle.

Chapter 19: Thoughts and Behavior

1 Martin Luther King, "Where Do We Go from Here?" Famous Speeches and Speech Topics, http://www.famous-speeches-and-speech-topics.info/martin-luther-king-speeches/martin-luther-king-speech-where-do-we-go-from-here.htm.

Chapter 20: The Mind-Mouth Connection

1 http://www.goodreads.com/quotes/29553-words-which-do-not-give-the-light-of-christ-increase.

Chapter 21: How to Get Your Mind Back When You Feel Like You Have Lost It!

1 Jane Austen, *Sense and Sensibility*, Vol. III (London: T. Egerton, 1811); available at https://archive.org/details/sensesensibility03aust.

JOYCE MEYER is one of the world's leading practical Bible teachers. Her TV and radio broadcast, *Enjoying Everyday Life*, airs on hundreds of television networks and radio stations worldwide.

Joyce has written more than one hundred inspirational books. Her best sellers include *Power Thoughts*; *The Confident Woman*; *Look Great, Feel Great*; *Starting Your Day Right*; *Ending Your Day Right*; *Approval Addiction*; *How to Hear from God*; *Beauty for Ashes*; and *Battlefield of the Mind*.

Joyce travels extensively, holding conferences throughout the year and speaking to thousands around the world.

Joyce Meyer Ministries—United States
P.O. Box 655
Fenton, MO 63026
USA
(636) 349-0303

Joyce Meyer Ministries—Canada
P.O. Box 7700
Vancouver, BC V6B 4E2
Canada
(800) 868-1002

Joyce Meyer Ministries—Australia
Locked Bag 77
Mansfield Delivery Centre
Queensland 4122
Australia
(07) 3349 1200

Joyce Meyer Ministries—England
P.O. Box 1549
Windsor SL4 1GT
United Kingdom
(0) 1753 831102

Joyce Meyer Ministries—South Africa
P.O. Box 5
Cape Town 8000
South Africa
(27) 21-701-1056

New Day, New You

The Penny

Perfect Love (previously published as *God Is Not Mad at You*)*

The Power of Being Positive

The Power of Being Thankful

The Power of Determination

The Power of Forgiveness

The Power of Simple Prayer

Power Thoughts

Power Thoughts Devotional

Reduce Me to Love

The Secret Power of Speaking God's Word

The Secrets of Spiritual Power

The Secret to True Happiness

Seven Things That Steal Your Joy

Start Your New Life Today

Starting Your Day Right

Straight Talk

Teenagers Are People Too!

Trusting God Day by Day

The Word, the Name, the Blood

Woman to Woman

You Can Begin Again

Joyce Meyer Spanish Titles

Belleza en Lugar de Cenizas (*Beauty for Ashes*)

Buena Salud, Buena Vida (*Good Health, Good Life*)

Cambia Tus Palabras, Cambia Tu Vida (*Change Your Words, Change Your Life*)

El Campo de Batalla de la Mente (*Battlefield of the Mind*)

Como Formar Buenos Habitos y Romper Malos Habitos (*Making Good Habits, Breaking Bad Habits*)

Dios No Está Enojado Contigo (*God Is Not Mad at You*)

La Dosis de Aprobación (*The Approval Fix*)

Empezando Tu Día Bien (*Starting Your Day Right*)

Hazte Un Favor a Ti Mismo…Perdona (*Do Yourself a Favor…Forgive*)

Madre Segura de sí Misma (*The Confident Mom*)

Pensamientos de Poder (*Power Thoughts*)

Perfecto Amor (*Perfect Love*)

Termina Bien tu Día (*Ending Your Day Right*)

Usted Puede Comenzar de Nuevo (*You Can Begin Again*)

Viva Valientemente (*Living Courageously*)

* Study Guide available for this title

Books By Dave Meyer

Life Lines

For more on the power of thoughts look for

BATTLEFIELD OF THE MIND
Winning *the Battle in Your Mind*
A multimillion bestseller

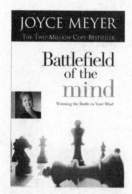

In her most popular book, Joyce Meyer explains how to transform negative thoughts that attack your mind so that you can enjoy a life of freedom, fruitfulness, and peace.

Also available in Spanish as *El Campo de Batalla de la Mente* and from hachette AUDIO and hachette DIGITAL

POWER THOUGHTS
12 Strategies to Win the Battle of the Mind

Joyce Meyer outlines twelve practical ways to use the mind as a tool for achievement—by turning thoughts into habits and habits into success.

Also available in Spanish as *Pensamientos de Poder* and from hachette AUDIO and hachette DIGITAL

Faith Words